WWW.ZODIACSERVICES.NET

RANGOLI / KOLAM / MUGGU HANDBOOK!

A SIMPLE HANDBOOK OF RANGOLI / KOLAM / MUGGU

HANDMADE RANGOLIS/ KOLAMS/ MUGGULU

Life Grows With Us!

SIMPLE & EASY WAY TO UNDERSTAND & DRAW THE BASICS OF RANGOLI/ KOLAM/ MUGGU EASILY IN IMAGE/PICTURE AND KEYWORDS WITH EFFECTIVE CHAPTERS!

By

G.R. Narasimhan

Welcome to Zodiac Services Rangoli/ Kolam/ Muggu techniques in brief with effective topics and additional special pictorial descriptions!

GOOD LUCK TO BE A GOOD RANGOLI/ KOLAM/ MUGGU EXPERT!

Copyright © 2019 by **G.R. Narasimhan**

All rights reserved. No part of this book/e-book may be reproduced, distributed or transmitted in any form or by any means, including photocopying, recording or other electronic or mechanical methods, without the prior written permission of the author, except in the case of brief quotations embodied in critical reviews and certain other non-commercial uses permitted by copyright law. For permission requests, write to the author, addressed "Attention: Author," at the address below.

Zodiac Services, Chennai, India

Get more contact details and numbers from:

www.zodiacservices.net [or] mail to info@zodiacservices.net

Ordering Information for hardcopies:

Quantity sales – Special discounts are available on quantity purchases by corporations, associations and others. For details, contact the author at the address above.

JULY 2019 – First Edition

Released and Published in Amazon India

****
Legal Disclaimer/ Notice

All the chapters, topics, discussions, statements, e-books/books and web contents including this Rangoli/Kolam either online or offline are under Rangoli/ Kolam category. This guide is recommended to get simple understanding and guidance of basic kolam/rangoli drawings for education purpose only. Readers are requested to apply their own knowledge or refer or consult their own tutors or masters before acting on any of the recommendations for examinations and related activities. Neither Zodiac services nor any of its promoters, members or author (if anyone) holds any responsibility of any losses/ liability incurred (if any/ if you end up in loss) by acting on the same as given to follow in presentations or examinations. We or Zodiac services, Chennai/India offices anywhere in the world, are not responsible for, and will not compensate in any way for, any loss or damage related directly or indirectly from/to the information on this book/e-book. Thanks for your cooperation!

****

ABOUT THE AUTHOR

G.R. Narasimhan – Sr. Consultant for technology and business under **Zodiac Services Chennai** (as on June 2019) which was started in 2010 to serve the people in alternative beliefs/therapies like astrological predictions, prayers, remedies, prasanam (divine words) and vedic guidance for short- or long-term problems, vaastu, numerology, gem stones, yantras, mantras or rituals (related areas), yoga, meditation, counseling and alternative therapies consulting. Business & education, soft skills/software/electronics & communication training & promotion, web designing, career counseling and Internet & social media marketing are additionally served. Assisting the entrepreneurship business for the above mentioned areas to serve better for the clients, **G.R. Narasimhan** also the author of few e-books called "A Simple guide to Vedic Astrology," "Inverted Universal Meditation & Engineering," "Secrets of Equity Stocks to make Millions," "Symbolic Meditation & Developing ESP", "MBA Basics in 24 Hours" and many other (are already available in Amazon) having extended experience in IT + Management areas developed website and online marketing using different business strategies and continue the service very well to extend further including this "Rangoli / Kolam / Muggu Handbook" concepts specifically based on the real world application oriented drawings applied overall in the everyday happenings. With the continuous extraordinary ability and skills in research and experience, he is able to explain and train/assist others with extended support and guidance by counseling/consulting effectively.

Great thanks and good luck for everyone reading this book on "Rangoli / Kolam Handbook" with almost all the areas of kolam/ rangoli designs & patterns individually or as a group. For any queries and feedback, you can contact directly via email to info@zodiacservices.net, info@astroservices.in or astronara@gmail.com.

CONTENTS

Topic	Page Numbers
Introduction	5
Chapter One—Basic Rangoli/ Kolams	11
Chapter Two—Medium Rangoli/ Kolams (Intermediate)	26
Chapter Three—Advanced Rangoli/ Kolams	49
Chapter Four—Extra Rangoli/ Kolams	84
Conclusion & Thanks Note!	105

INTRODUCTION

Rangoli/ Kolam (or Muggu) – A conventional Indian adornment and examples made with ground rice, especially during celebrations. Rangoli is gotten from the Sanskrut word 'rangavalli'. Rangoli is a craftsmanship which goes before figure and painting. It is both a promising and a starter need in any religious custom. It is a custom to draw rangoli at the site of any promising religious custom, for example, a blessed celebration, a religious celebration, a propitious capacity like wedding, ceremonial love, a pledged religious recognition, and so on.

Rangoli is a fine art, beginning in the Indian subcontinent, in which examples are made on the floor or the ground utilizing materials, for example, hued rice, dry flour, shaded sand or blossom petals. It is generally made during Diwali or Tihar, Onam, Pongal and other Hindu celebrations in the Indian subcontinent. Plans are passed starting with one age then onto the next, keeping both the work of art and the custom alive. Generally in temples, home, celebrations, pooja rooms, marriages, birthdays or any other important places; rangolis are drawn.

The reason for rangoli is enhancement, and it is thought to bring good karma. Structure delineations may likewise differ as they reflect conventions, old stories, and practices that are interesting to every territory. It is customarily done by young ladies or ladies. For the most part, this training is displayed during events, for example, celebrations, favorable observances, marriage festivities and other comparative achievements and get-togethers.

Rangoli structures can be basic geometric shapes, god impressions, or blossom and petal shapes (proper for the given festivals), however they can likewise be intricate plans made by various individuals. The base material is typically dry or wet powdered rice or dry flour, to which sindoor (vermilion), haldi (turmeric) and other regular hues can be included.

Different materials incorporate shaded sand, red block powder and even blooms and petals, as on account of blossom rangolis.

In center India mostly Rangoli is called Chaook and is commonly drawn at the passageway of a house or some other structure. Dried rice flour or different types of white residue powder is utilized for illustration Chaooks. Despite the fact that there are various conventional Chaook designs, a lot more can be made relying upon the imagination of the individual who draws it. It is viewed as favorable as it implies showering of good karma and success on the house and in the family. It isn't drawn like an image.

Examples are made dependent on specific frameworks. For the most part, ladies rise promptly in the first part of the day and clean the territory simply outside the passage of their homes with dairy animals compost, sprinkle the zone with water and draw the Chaook. In Maharashtra and Karnataka, rangolis are drawn on the entryways of homes so abhorrent powers endeavoring to enter are repulsed.

During the celebration of Onam in Kerala, blooms are set down for every one of the ten days of the festival, the plan becoming bigger and increasingly complex consistently. In Tamil Nadu, Andhra Pradesh and Karnataka,and numerous pieces of Maharashtra, the Rangoli or Kolam is drawn upon the ground or floor day by day.

The Rangoli designs generally are committed to Lord Krishna and Lord Jagannath. The Murja celebration is seen during the promising month of Kartika finishing on Kartika Purnima.

The Rangoli's most significant component is being beautiful. These are propitious images that have a focal job in the plan. The plan for ages are passed on as they are made – and is required to make these images. Customarily, each new age learns the workmanship and in this way a family keeps the convention flawless. Some significant images utilized in Rangoli are the lotus blossom, its leaves, mango, Tue vase, fish, distinctive sort of flying creatures like parrots, swans, peacocks, and human figures and foliage. Regularly Rangoli is made on uncommon events like Diwali. Some exceptional examples for Diwali Rangoli are the Diya additionally called Deep, Ganesha, Lakshmi, blooms or flying creatures of India.

The second key component is utilizing the materials used to make the rangoli. The materials utilized are effectively found all over the place. Accordingly, this craftsmanship is predominant in all homes, rich or poor. Ordinarily the significant fixings used to make rangoli are – Pise rice arrangement, the dried powder produced using the leaves shading, charcoal, consumed soil was, wood sawdust, and so on.

The third significant component is the foundation. Rangoli utilize the foundation of an unmistakable floor or divider or Llype is utilized. Rangoli can be made in a yard in the center, corners, or as a chime is made around.

Dehri passage is a custom of making rangoli. God's seat, contingent upon light, spot of love and penance on the special stepped area is a custom of improving rangoli. With time, creative mind and inventive thoughts in Rangoli workmanship is likewise fused. Cordiality and the travel industry has likewise had its impact and rangoli has been financially created in spots, for example, lodgings. Its customary appeal, imaginativeness significance still remain.

Rangoli is additionally made utilizing hued rice, dry flour, blossom petals, turmeric (haldi), Vermillion (Sindoor) and hued sand. The examples incorporate the substance of Hindu divinities, geometric shapes peacock themes, and round botanical plans. A significant number of these themes are customary and are passed on by the past ages. This makes rangoli a portrayal of India's rich legacy and the way that it is a place where there is celebrations and shading. Individuals celebrate rangoli with davali designs.

There are two essential approaches to make a Rangoli, dry and wet, alluding to the materials used to make the diagram and (whenever wanted) fill that blueprint with shading. Utilizing a white material like chalk, sand, paint or flour, the craftsman denotes a middle point on the ground and cardinal focuses around it, normally in a square, hexagon or hover contingent upon locale and individual inclination.

Ramifying that at first straightforward example makes what is frequently a multifaceted and delightful structure. Themes from nature (leaves, petals, plumes) and geometric examples are normal. Less normal yet in no way, shape or form uncommon are illustrative structures (like a peacock, symbol or scene). "Readymade Rangoli" designs, frequently as stencils or stickers, are getting to be normal, making it simpler to make exact structures.

When the layout is finished, the craftsman may light up it with shading, again utilizing either wet or dry fixings like paints, hued rice-water, gypsum powder, hued sand or dry colors. The craftsman may likewise pick natural materials like seeds, grains, flavors, leaves or bloom petals to accomplish similar tones.

Present day materials like pastels, colors or colored textures, acrylic paints and fake shading specialists are additionally getting to be normal, taking into consideration splendid and lively shading decisions. A fresher yet less fake technique includes utilizing concrete hued with marble powder. This fairly exact strategy requires preparing, however delightful pictures can be attracted this medium.

Shape, structure and material can be affected by territorial customs. A square network is regular in North India just like a hexagonal framework in South India; Onam Rangolis are commonly roundabout.

In North India, the shading is frequently founded on gypsum (chirodi), in South India on rice flour and Onam Rangolis are commonly blossom based. The quick and far reaching relocation and blending of individuals inside India can be seen by the manner in which these styles are presently unreservedly embraced and blended the nation over.

It is likewise getting to be basic to see experimentation like sawdust-based coasting Rangolis, freestyle plans, and intriguing materials. It is especially eminent that the Tamil rendition of the Rangoli, the Kolam, prizes symmetry, multifaceted nature, accuracy, and unpredictability as opposed to the flashiness of Rangolis found in North India.

Numerous individuals think that its pleasant to attempt to make sense of how such complex plans are drawn with a matrix, and henceforth, it enables the psyche to be worked out. In Tamil Nadu, there is a predominant fantasy, that Andaal loved Lord Thirumaal and was hitched to him in the period of Margazhi. So during this month, unmarried young ladies get up before first light and attract a Rangoli to respect the god Thirumal.

Notices of rangoli creation are likewise found in Hindu folklore. See likewise references to Rangoli in legend, for example, in the – Ramayana at Sita's wedding structure where the dialog alludes to rangoli there. Social advancement of Rangoli in the South started in the time of the Chola Rulers. There are current and conventional rangoli plans. The plans are generally motivated essentially, however they can likewise be as dynamic workmanship.

More benefits of Kolam/Rangoli: It is viewed as favorable to attract rangoli Hindu Dharma during uncommon events and religious services. Rangolis are accepted to have otherworldly point of view and advantages. It is said that with the difference in shading, structure and structure, the vibration of a rangoli changes.

Making Rangoli is a workmanship and numerous individuals love to make it. In such a way, the primary significant preferred position of making Rangoli is that you feel positive while making it and this procedure diminishes your pressure.

When you make Rangoli, your fingers and thumbs combine and make Gyan mudra, which makes your mind vigorous and dynamic just as assume a significant job in scholarly advancement.

This stance is successful for your wellbeing even in pressure point massage. It shields you from hypertension and gives mental and otherworldly harmony.

The positive and negative impacts of hues have been considered by science and different therapeutic practices. When you interact with the hues, the vitality radiated by them influences you, which is conceivable to treat numerous kinds of mental and physical issues.

Rangoli, produced using various hues and blooms makes positive vitality in your home and environment. It makes the mind wonderful and the climate ends up positive. It additionally influences your wellbeing.

Rangoli/Kolams are universal patterns in many cases if you observe closely. Mind is able to catch many positive patterns naturally when rangoli is drawn by the universal law of attraction and shape up in a creative direction. It improves creativity, confidence, will power, concentration, art skills and many.

There are two major types of Rangoli/ Kolam:

1. Dotted pattern
2. Free Pattern

Dotted pattern starts by keeping dots to connect lines in rangoli/ kolam. Free patterns are without dots and the rangoli maker can start mostly from center of the kolam as per their wish. Dots are just to give perfection of lines and patters.

This book is released for 100+ simple(basic), medium(intermediate) & advanced sized rangolis/ kolams which are drawn for different occasions like Diwali, Sankranthi, Ganesh Chadurthi, Ugadhi, New Year, Temple festivals etc. These kolams are not printed one; they are drawn simply with freehand.

Most of the rangoli/ kolams/ muggus in this handbook are drawn with free hand in the paper or notebooks. Many others are down on the floor in our houses and temples as well. So nothing is computer generated design here. Naturally it has been pictured and cropped wherever necessary and brief description given for these designs.

Good Luck!

"Drawing Patterns of Rangoli/ Kolam shape up the mind to think creatively and execute the tasks well from the universal pattern; improves sub conscious mind power that lead to stress free life"

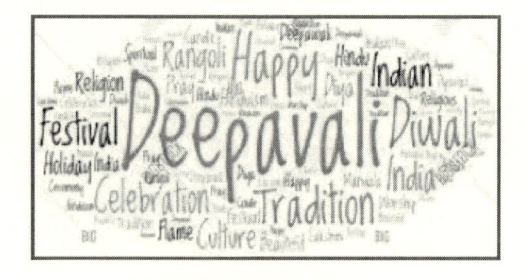

Chapter One - Basic Patterns
1

- This is free hand drawing rangoli or kolam. Starting from the curved square box from the center and a small circle; the rest of curved patters are drawn. No dots are used here. So it is a free pattern kolam.

- This is also called as padi kolam padi muggu in some texts and it is simple and easy way of drawing with different combinations.

Search "**Secrets of Gayatri mantras and moola mantras**" in Kindle or Amazon to download for greater chanting/ auspicious poojas!

Author: "G R Narasimhan"

2

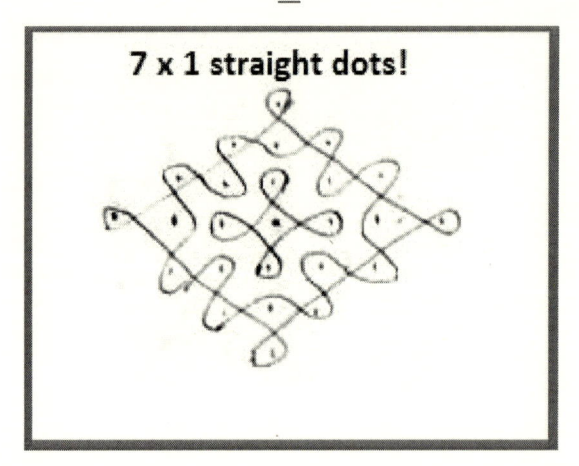

7 x 1 straight dots!

- Simple kolam starts with 7 dots in the middle and 5, 3, 1 dots in straight in all the sided or top and bottom.
- Then from the middle you have to draw the free curved lines.

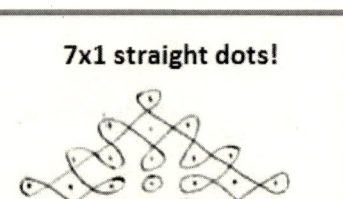

3

7x1 straight dots!

- This Rangoli/ Simple kolam starts with 7 dots in the middle and 5, 3, 1 dots in straight in all the sided or top and bottom same as above.
- Then from the middle you have to draw the circle and other free curved lines.

4

Simple hexogen in the middle and form the rest!

- The above one is simple hexogen shaped center and then star drawn above. The followed by flower shaped designs in each corner. No dots required.

5

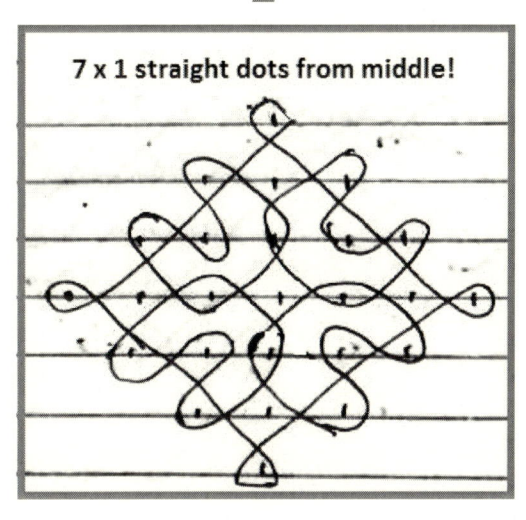

7 x 1 straight dots from middle!

- 7 dots in the middle row and then followed by 5, 3, 1 dots either side or all sides. Then the pattern starts with freehand drawing from center.

6

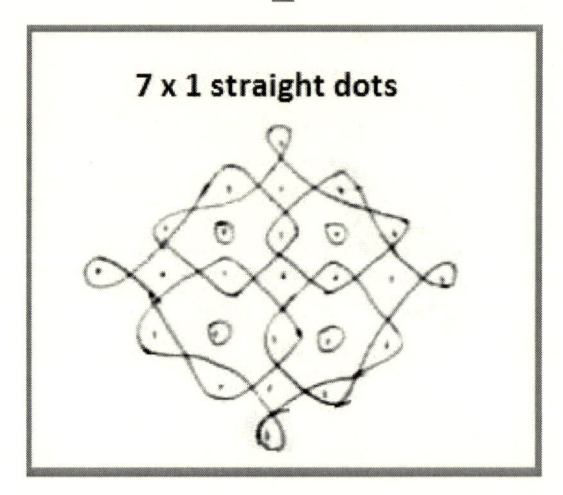

7 x 1 straight dots

- The above one 7 is also 7 dots in the middle and then 5, 3, 1 dots in the sides and then drawn freehand with curved lines.

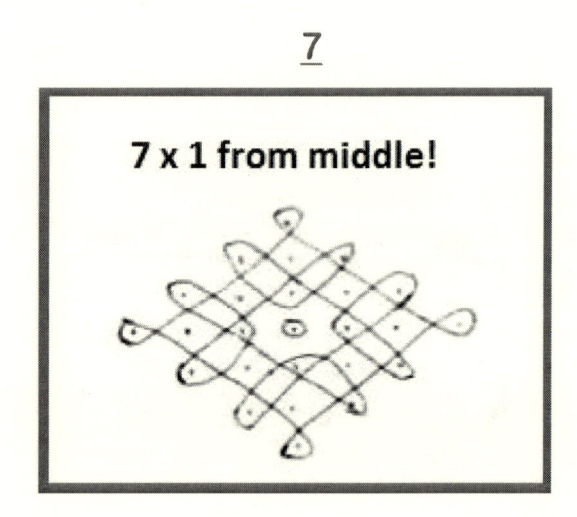

7

7 x 1 from middle!

- This kolam is also similar dotted pattern; but only the lines are in different style/design.

8

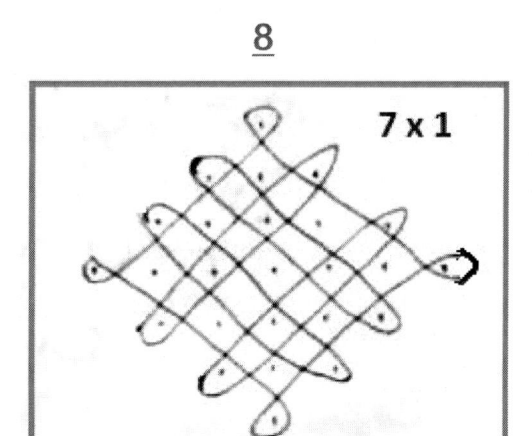

[7 x 1]

- This one again uses 7, 5, 3, 1 dots in straight lines and then the easy long connecting lines forms simple shapes.

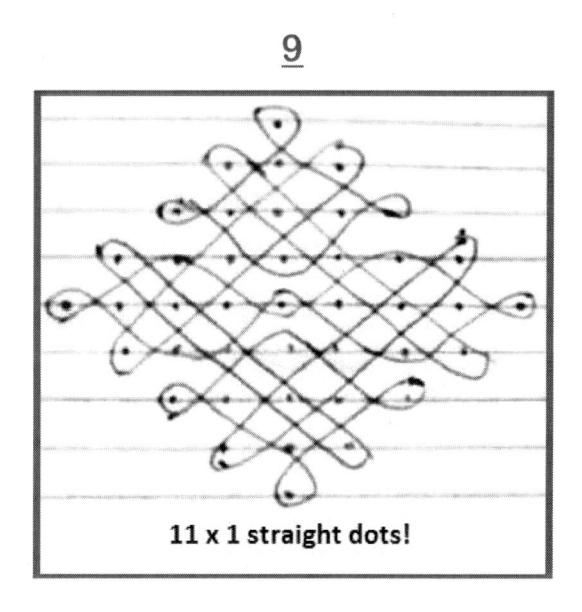

9

11 x 1 straight dots!

- This kolam is a similar to the previous designs; but 9 dots in the middle followed by 7, 5, 3, 1 dots in the top and bottom sides. Then the free hand lines are drawn which are creating each dot in a container.

10

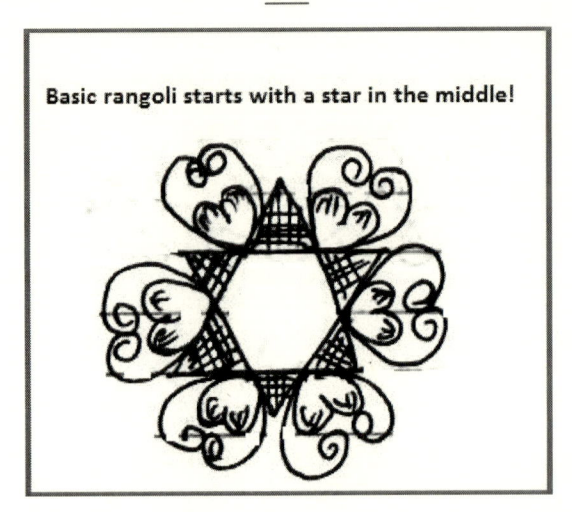

Basic rangoli starts with a star in the middle!

- The above one is again a simple hexogen shaped center and then star drawn above hexogen. The followed by heart/flower shaped designs in each corner intersection of hexogen. No dots required.

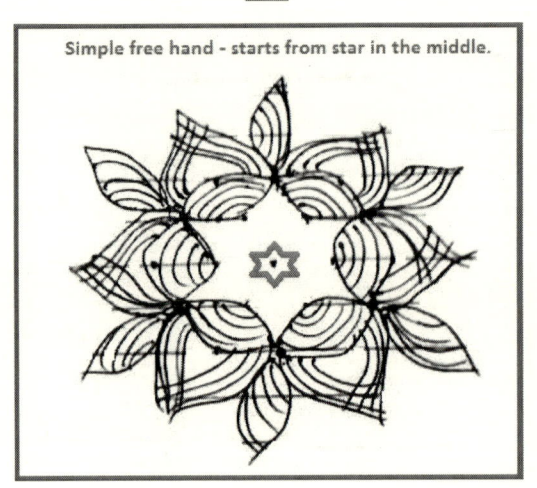

11

Simple free hand - starts from star in the middle.

- Star shaped design in the middle and then another bigger star in outer area. Then the other designs are drawn to form petal shapes.

12

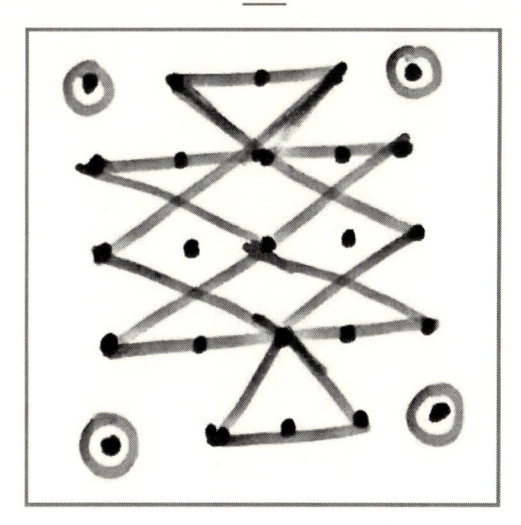

- 5 x 5 dots in straight lines and then the shapes are formed accordingly. Simple design to have triangle and circle shapes.

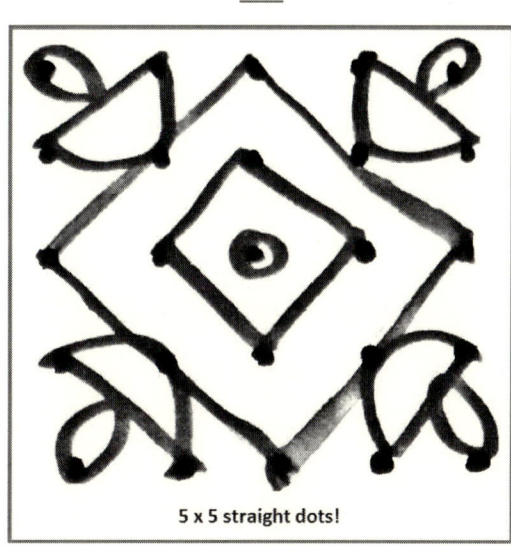

13

5 x 5 straight dots!

- Similar as above 5 x 5 dots in straight lines and then the shapes are formed accordingly. Simple design to have diamond shapes and lamp shapes each side.

14

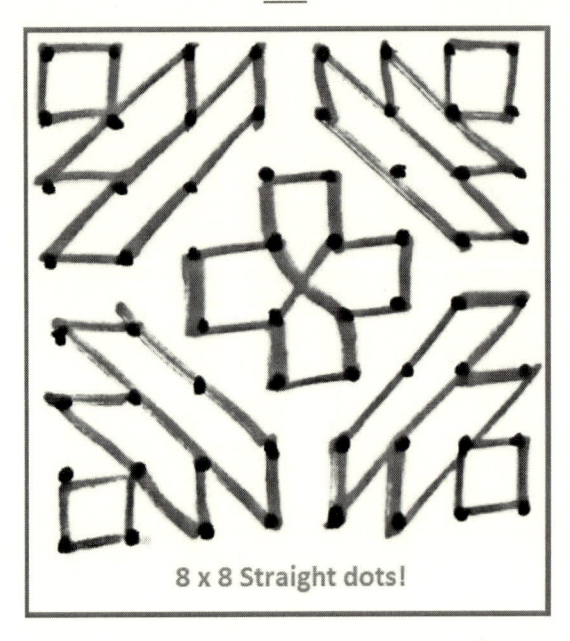

8 x 8 Straight dots!

- Basically 8 x 8 dots are kept in rows and then a cross drawn in the middle followed by square shapes. Then lamp designs are formed in each corner by connecting the dots.

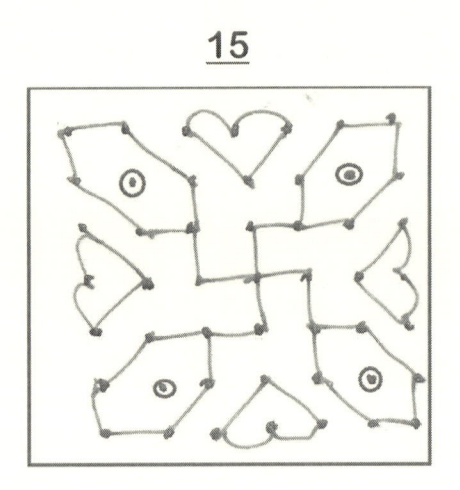

15

- 7 x 7 dots formation of a plus / swasthic symbol in center and then heart shape and hexogen shapes are around.

16

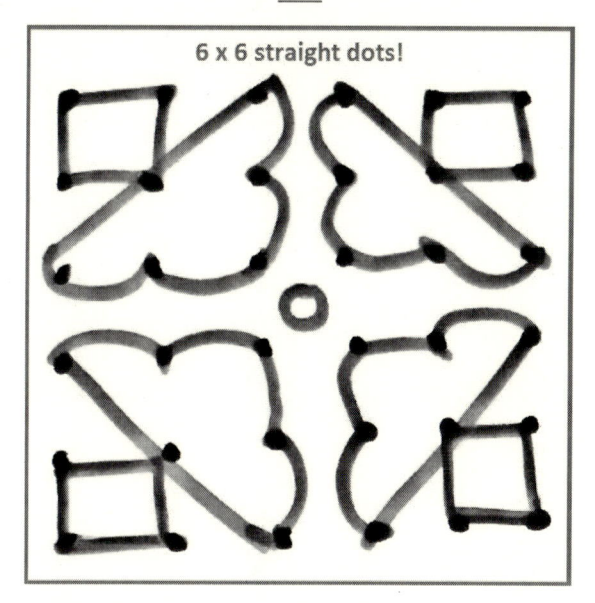

6 x 6 straight dots!

- 6 x 6 dots in straight and draw lamp or flower pot designs towards the corners.

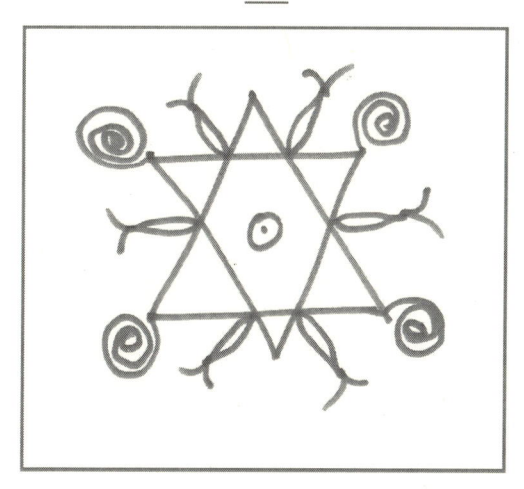

17

- First form six faces star and then the other designs. No dots required. This can be extended to any shape.

18

7 x 7 straight dots!

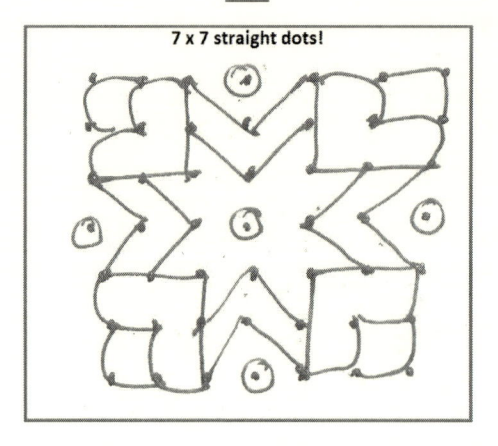

- 7 x 7 above dots forms 8 faces star in the middle and then connect heart shaped designs cross corner. Free dots are covered by small circles.

19

- Four lines intersecting in the middle forms 8 lines in 360 degrees. Then the shapes drawn. No dots required in general. Can be extended to any design.

20

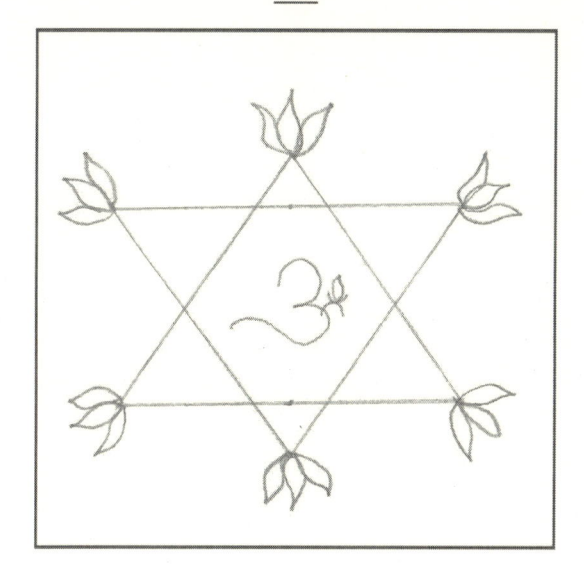

- Six faces; star shaped lines in the middle and flower petals or lamp drawn in each corner.

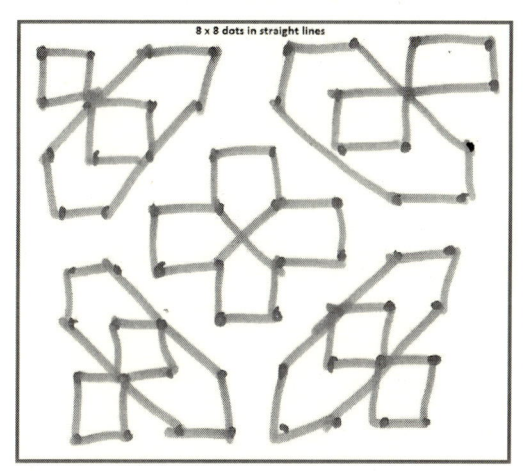

21

- Another 8 x 8 dots with different design.

22

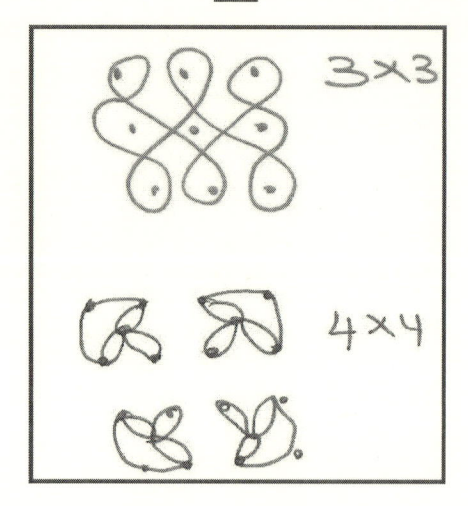

- 3 x 3 and 4 x 4 simple design kolams to form basic shapes.

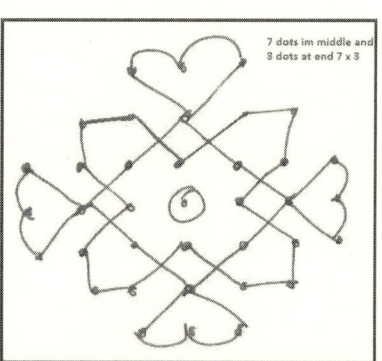

23

- 7 dots in 3 middle rows; then 5 and 3 in top and bottom. Then form the shapes with free hand lines.

24

Star shape in the the middle and draw rest!

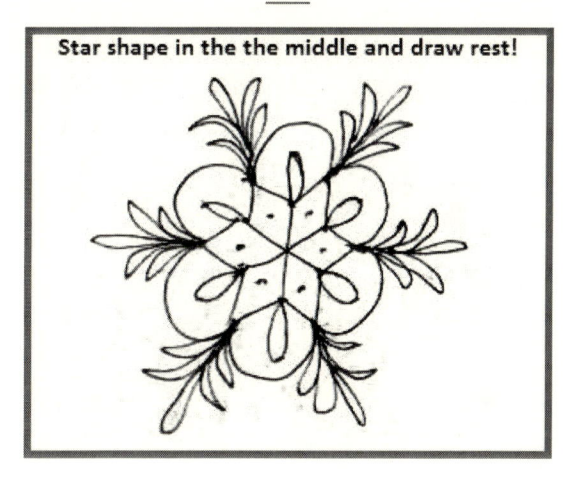

- 6 faces; star shaped design in the middle and then the plant like drawing is made. No dots required. Dots are for decorative purpose only.

25

- 9 x 1 straight dots from middle to top/bottom. Starting from middle the heart shaped pattern drawn and then flower shaped pattern in the outer.

26

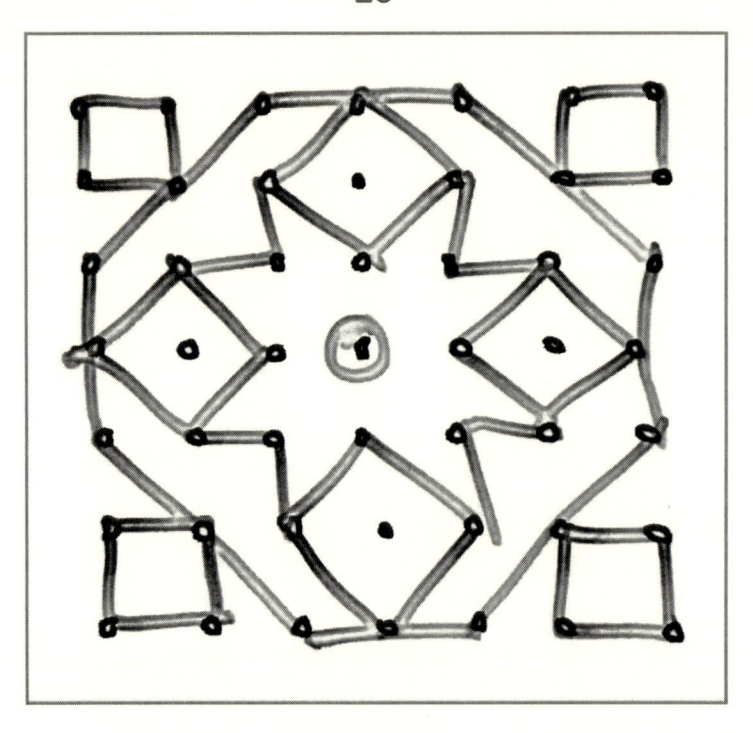

- 7 x 7 straight dots to create star pattern in the middle and then diamond outer. Small squares are in the corners.

27

- 7 x 1 simple diamond and heart shapes at the end. Starting from the middle to top/bottom.

28

- 8 x 8 straight dots forming small cross in the middle and then followed by other outer shapes/ triangles in the corner.

Search "Secrets of Gayatri mantras and moola mantras" in Kindle or Amazon to download for greater chanting/ auspicious poojas!

Author: "G R Narasimhan"

Chapter Two - Medium Patterns (Intermediate)

This chapter is giving medium basic or semi advanced rangolis/ kolams for practice.

1

7, 9 x 2 straight dots from middle!

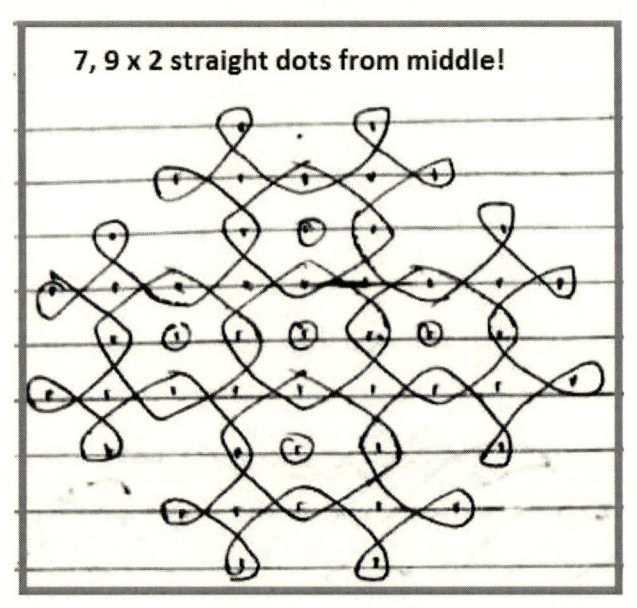

- 7 dots in the middle row and then 9 dots above and below. Then 5 and 2 dots by skipping few dots to form star or diamond shapes with free hand lines. All are straight dots only.

2

11 x 6 interlaced dots from middle!

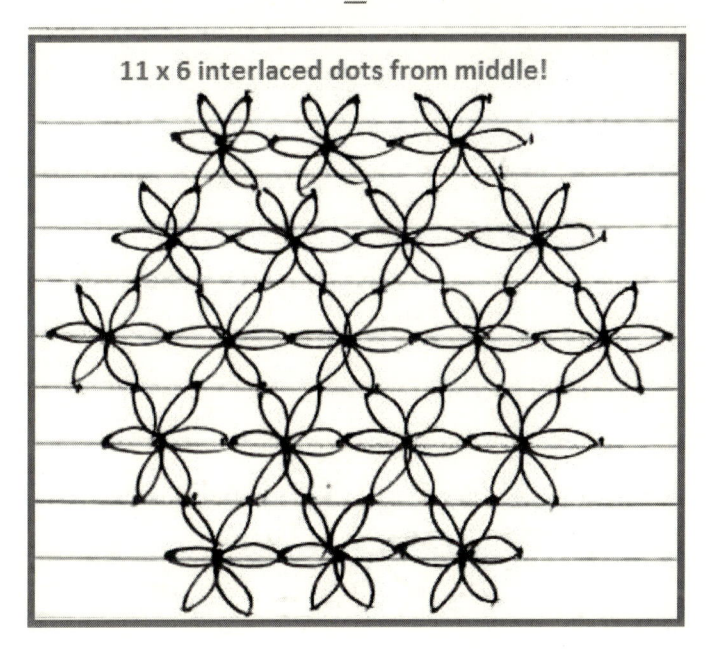

- 11 dots in the middle and then 10, 9, 8 ……6 dots above and below in each row. Interlaced dots forming flower shaped designed by connecting each row dots.

3

8 x 2 straight dots from middle!

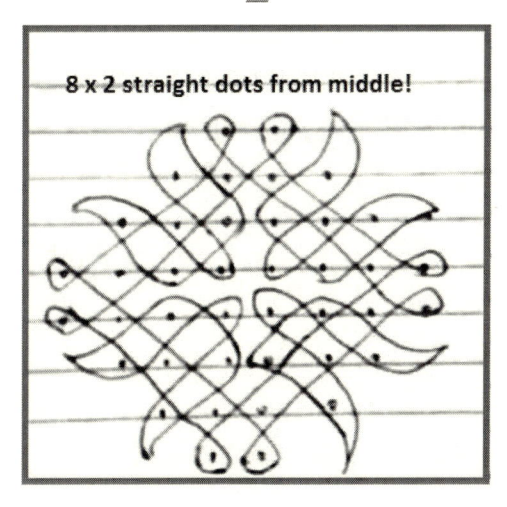

- 8 dots in 2 middle rows and ending up with 2 dots in in all the sides. Then the free drawn lines are forming even shapes.

4

11 x 1 interlaced dots!

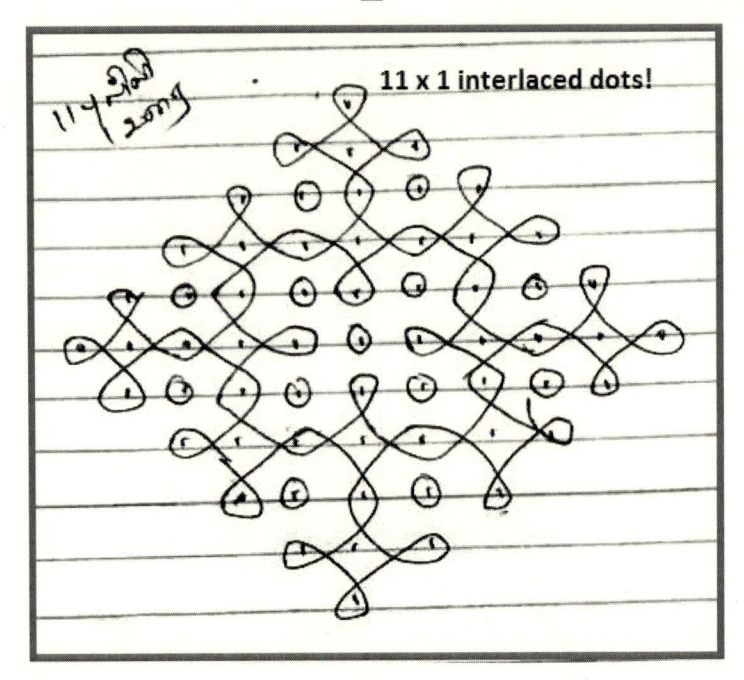

- 11 x 1 (11, 9, 7, 5, 3 and 1) dots in straight lines; from the middle. Then a small circle in the center and then other shapes are formed.

- Free dots are covered by small circles.

5

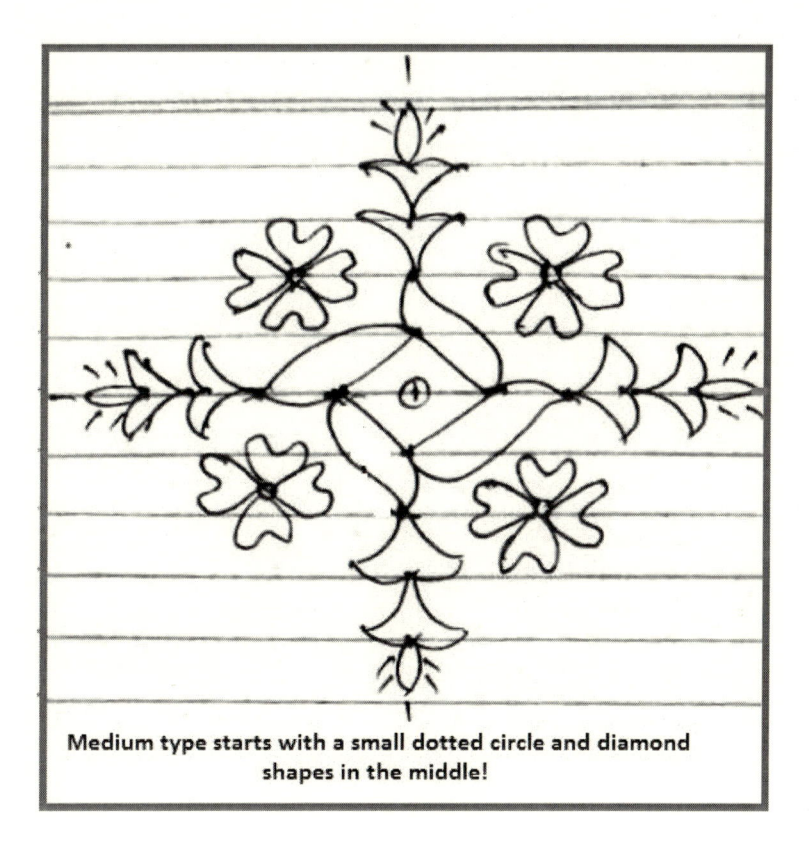

Medium type starts with a small dotted circle and diamond shapes in the middle!

- 11 or 9 dots in 3 rows in the middle (forms a cross +) then the shapes are drawn simply like free hand curve.

6

Medium type starts with a small circle and flower in the middle!

- No dots are required here. Just draw a small flower design in the middle and then connecting lamp like shape surrounded. Finally peacock like shapes are drawn.

Search "Secrets of Gayatri mantras and moola mantras" in Kindle or Amazon to download for greater chanting/ auspicious poojas!

Author: "G R Narasimhan"

7

Free hand - Medium type starts from star in the middle

- This rangoli is free hand star drawing in the middle. Then some cross likes in between the faces of star. Lotus like shapes are formed from the corners of the triangle.

Search "Secrets of Gayatri mantras and moola mantras" in Kindle or Amazon to download for greater chanting/ auspicious poojas!

Author: "G R Narasimhan"

8

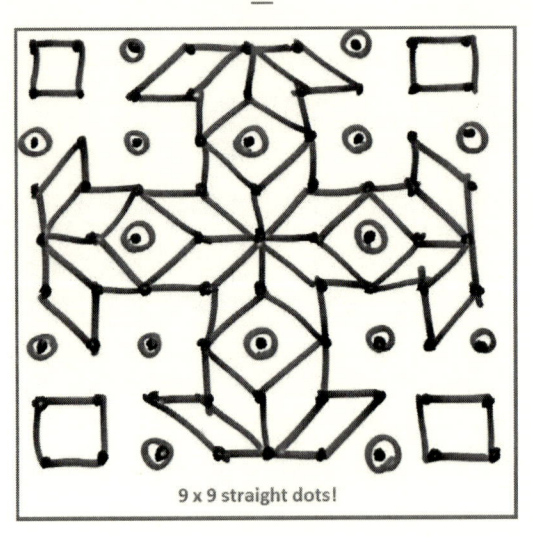

9 x 9 straight dots!

- 8 x 8 straight dots are in rows and columns. Four square shaped designs are drawn in the corners. Then 8 faces star shape is drawn followed by other design patterns.

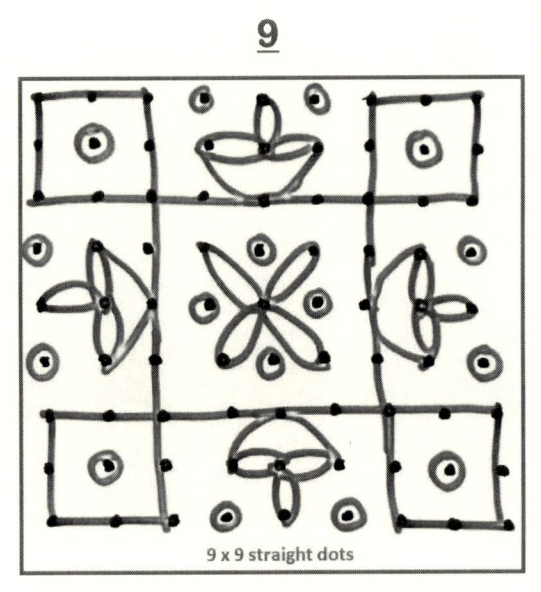

9

9 x 9 straight dots

- 8 x 8 straight dots are in rows and columns. Small flower shape in the middle and square & lamp shapes are drawn.

10

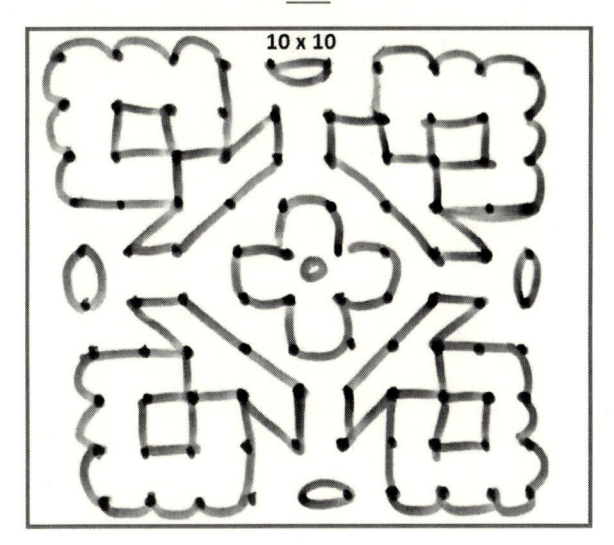

- 10 x 10 straight dots are in rows and columns. Starting from the middle all the shapes are formed as shown above.

11

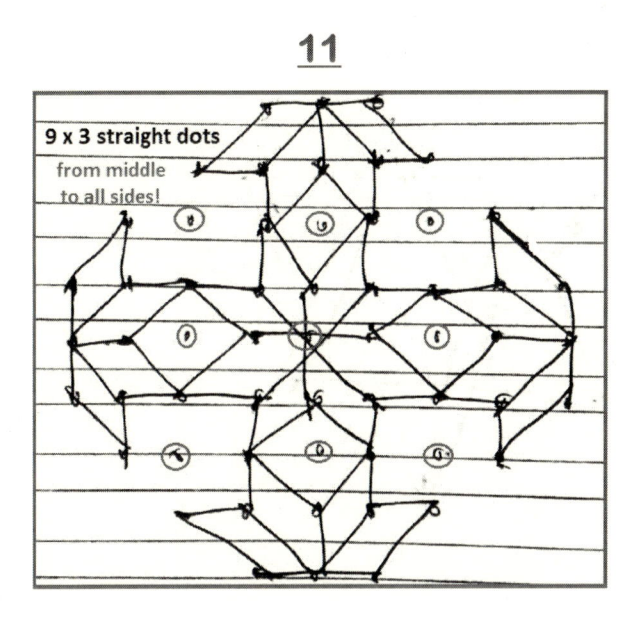

- 9 dots in 3 rows from the middle in cross and then ending up with 3 dots all sides. Medium basic lines are formed from the center and completed in all the directions.

12

15 x 8 interlaced dots!

- 15 dots in the middle row and then interlaced dots to top and bottom ending 8. Then star shaped formation from the center and "Sangu" shapes are drawn all sides.

13

- Above one is free hand drawing without dots. From center, star shape starts and then rest of curved lines drawn. (Also called padi kolam)

14

13 x 7 interlaced dots!

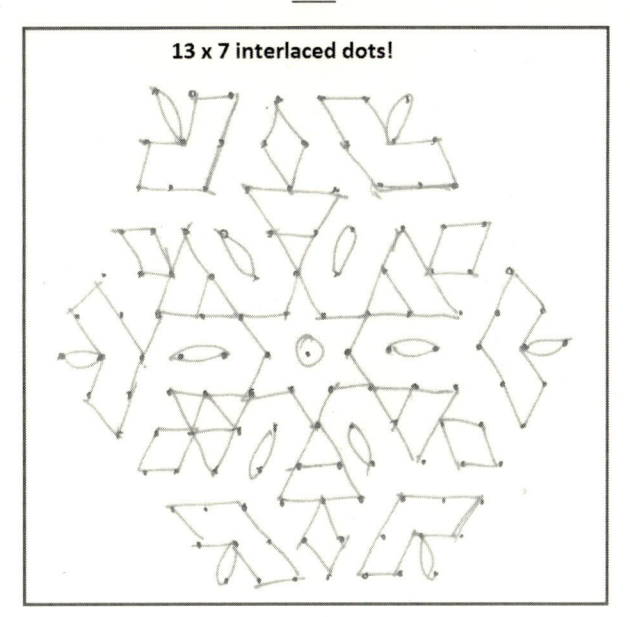

- This is 13 dots in the middle and then interlaced dots till reaching top and bottom. Then the lines drawn to form shapes from the center star.

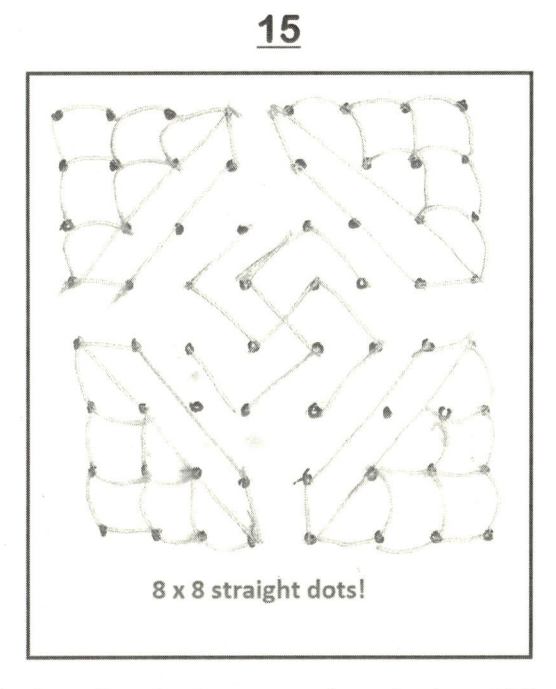

15

8 x 8 straight dots!

- 8 x 8 straight dots directly gives cross shape in the middle and then the rest of shapes.

16

11x6 interlaced dots! middle to top/bottom.

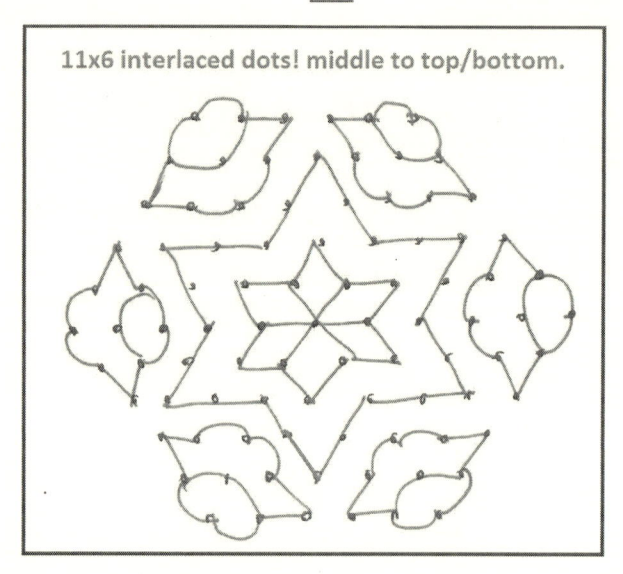

- 11 x 6 from the middle to top/bottom. Middle star shapes and then followed by "Sangu" shapes around.

17

12 x 1 interlaced dots! middle to top/bottom!

- Above all sangu shapes are drawn by 12 x 1 interlaced dots from the middle.

18

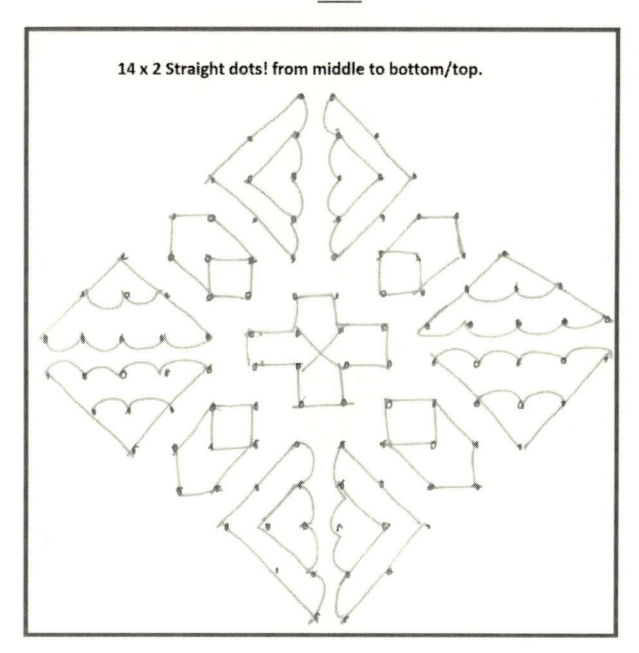

14 x 2 Straight dots! from middle to bottom/top.

- 14 dots in two rows in the middle horizontally and vertically. Then ending with 2 dots with straight pattern. Cross shape in the middle and then others are covered up.

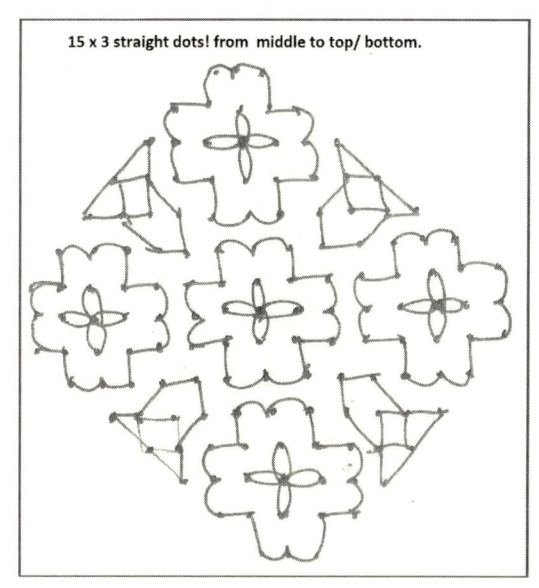

19

15 x 3 straight dots! from middle to top/ bottom.

- 15 straight dots in 3 rows horizontally and vertically from the middle and then ending up with 3 dots all sides. Shapes are drawn from middle.

20

15 x 1 straight dots! from middle to top/ bottom.

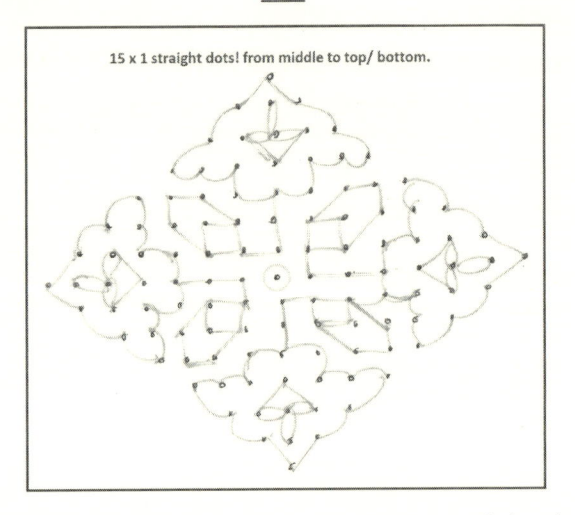

- 15 x 1 straight dots ending up with 1 dot all sides and the shapes are drawn from the center.

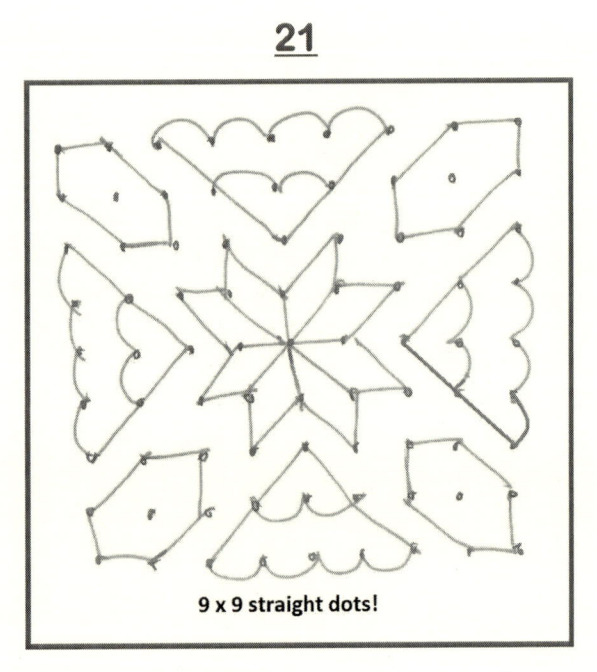

21

9 x 9 straight dots!

- Above is 9 x 9 dots in straight line to get the star shape in the middle and bird shapes in four sides. Diamond shapes are formed in the corners.

22

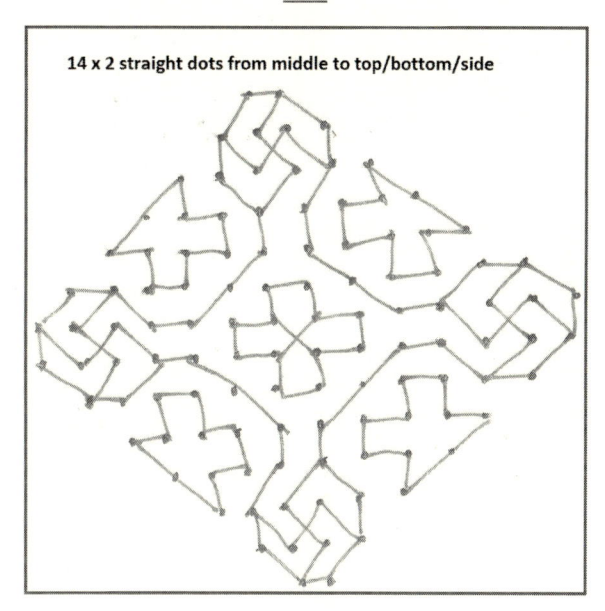

14 x 2 straight dots from middle to top/bottom/side

- Simple medium type 14 x 2 straight dots formation. Just a cross in the middle and other lines are connected to form shapes.

23

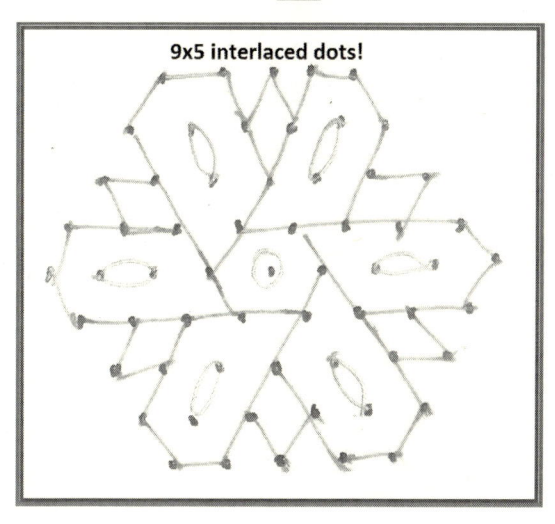

9x5 interlaced dots!

- 9 x 5 interlaced dots forming hexagonal shapes from the center. Free dots are connected for elliptical shapes.

24

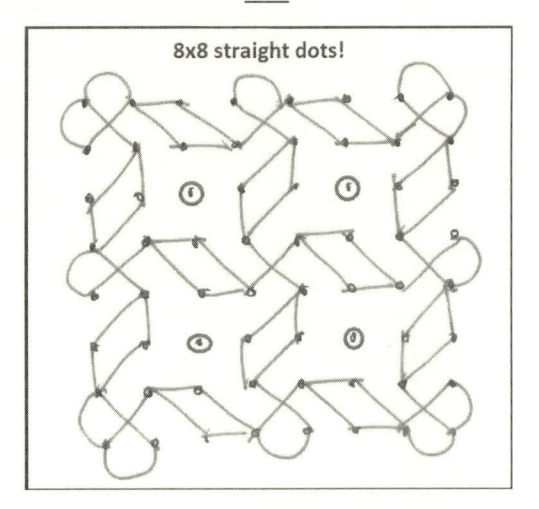

- 8 x 8 straight line dots; first a simple X symbol from the middle is extended to form various diamond shapes around. Then semi circular design to cover the surroundings.

25

- Medium complex with 10 x 10 straight dots. Cross lines from the middle and rest of the design patterns are drawn.

26

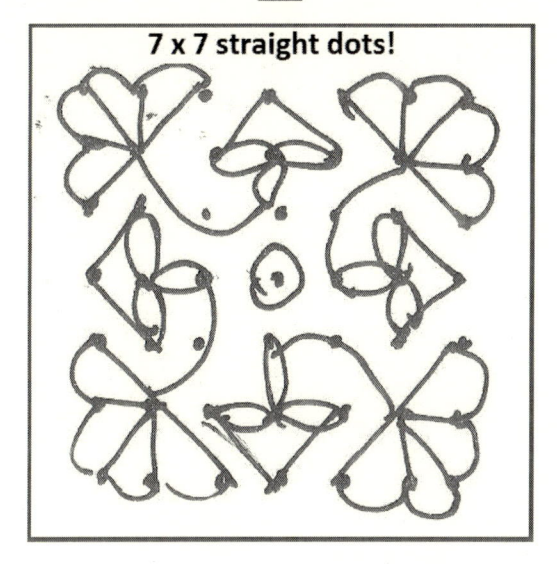

- Above is 7 x 7 dots in straight lines are arranged to draw different lamp and flower shapes.

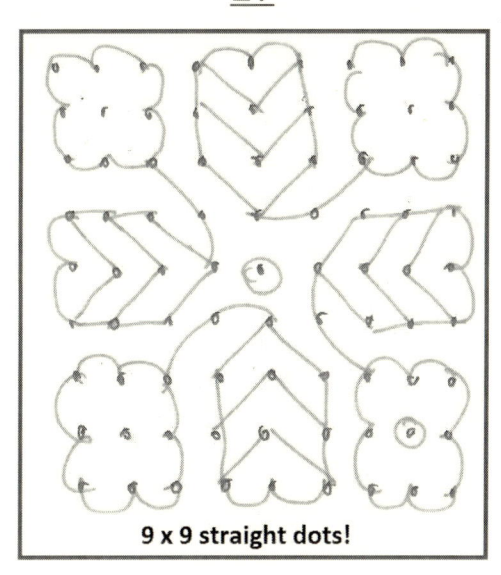

27

- Here 9 x 9 straight dots are arranged to form flower pots with flowers.

28

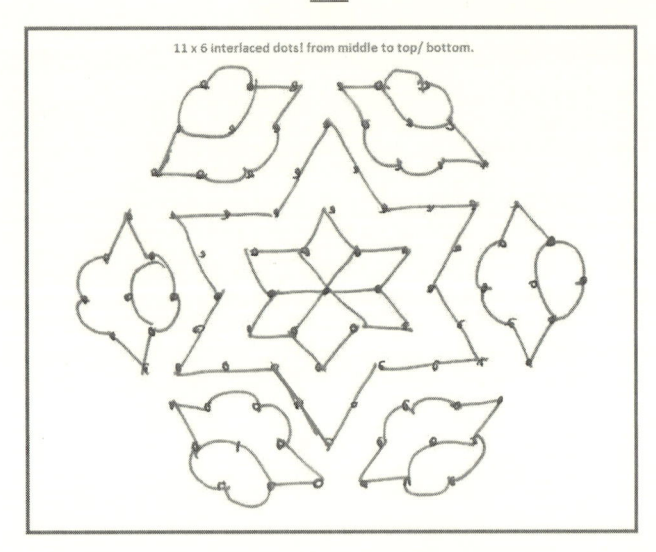

- 11 x 6 interlaced dots from the middle to top/bottom. Stars from the middle and bowl shape/ flowers around.

29

- 11 x 1 straight dots from the middle to top/bottom. From the center various shapes are drawn. Free dots are covered by circles.

30

11 x 6 interlaced points! From middle to top & bottom rows.

- 11 x 6 interlaced dots are from the middle to top/bottom. Simple lines from the middle followed by curved lines and finally ending up with triangle shapes.

31

- Freehand medium drawn rangoli/ kolam above with 6 faces; star shaped lines and semi circular lines are further extended to finish with curved designs. (Another padi kolam type)

32

- Another freehand medium drawn rangoli/ kolam above with 8 faces of star shaped lines inner and outer from the center. Lines are further extended to finish with bird shaped designs. (Another padi kolam type)

33

- Simple medium freehand drawing with circles in the center and then formed a star. Then extended to draw bell flower shaped finishing.

34

- Medium advanced freehand drawing with curves in the center and then formed 4 curved triangles. Corners are covered with flower designs.

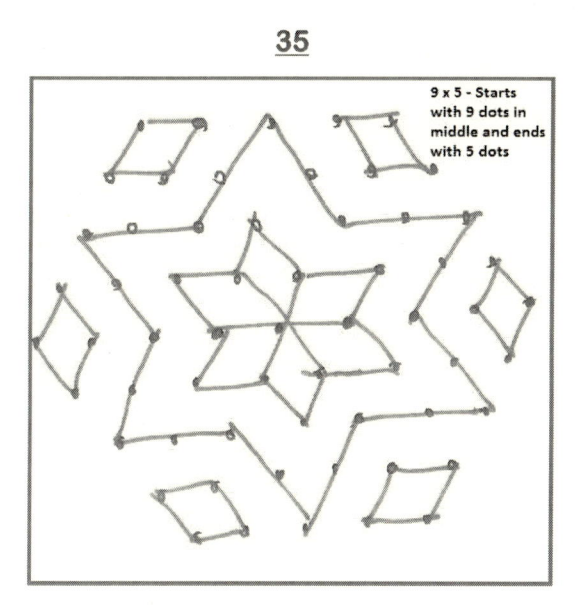

35

9 x 5 - Starts with 9 dots in middle and ends with 5 dots

- 9 x 5 interlaced dots to form star and diamond shapes in and around. Simple medium type starts with 9 dots to 5 dots from center to top/bottom.

36

15 x 3 direct dots

Indicates "Welcome" in Tamil

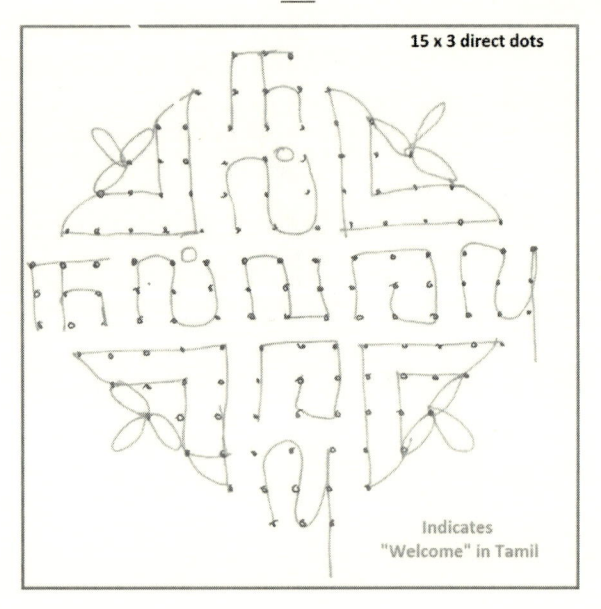

- This indicates "Welcome" in tamil language. Uses 15 x 3 straight dots in all sides (middle 3 lines are 15 dots). Corners are decorated with lamps.

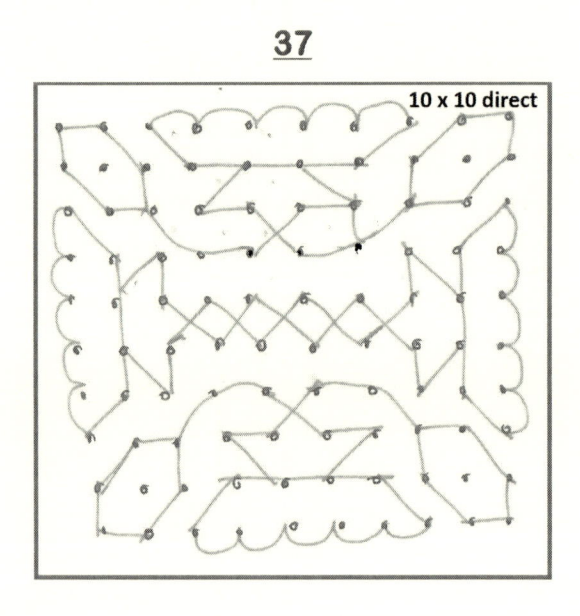

37

10 x 10 direct

- 10 x 10 straight dots are connected to form lamp shaped images.

38

11 x 6 interlaced dots!

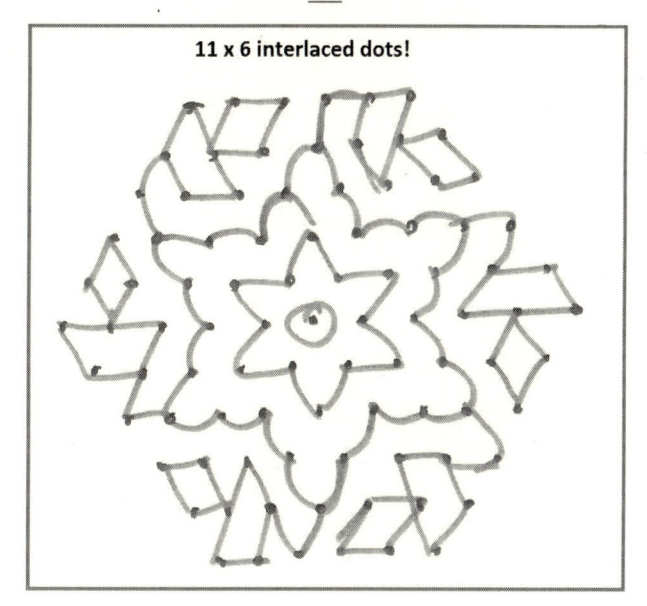

- 11 x 6 interlaced dots from the middle to top/bottom. Center star formation first and then outer design with curved/ straight lines to form lamps.

39

- Simple medium 4 lines are drawn in the middle across to make 8 lines and connected as star. Then other shapes drawn.

40

Circle and flower shapes in the middle and then draw!

- Freehand medium type rangoli is shown above. First 2 circles in the center and then flower shape is drawn. Then other designs were completed.

41

- 9 x 9 dots in straight line. Starting from the center, a small flower shaped pattern in the middle and then different types of lamps in all the directions.

Chapter Three - Advanced Patterns

This chapter gives little bit extra work for the people who practice rangoli or kolam. Additional effort needed which compare to basic and medium (intermediate) types.

1

11 x 1 straight dots from middle!

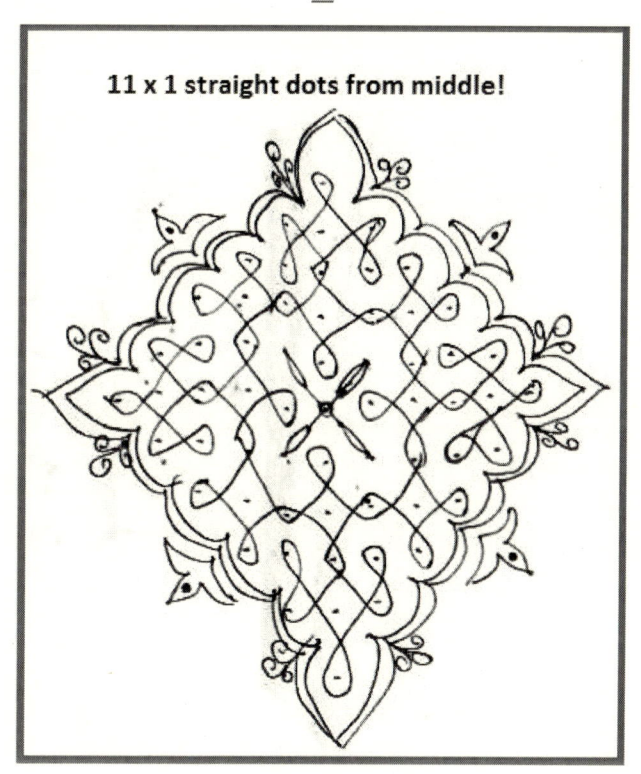

- Above rangoli is formed with 11 x 1 straight dots to form the entire shape. After finishing the curved lines to finish the dotted designs, then the outer pattern drawn.

2

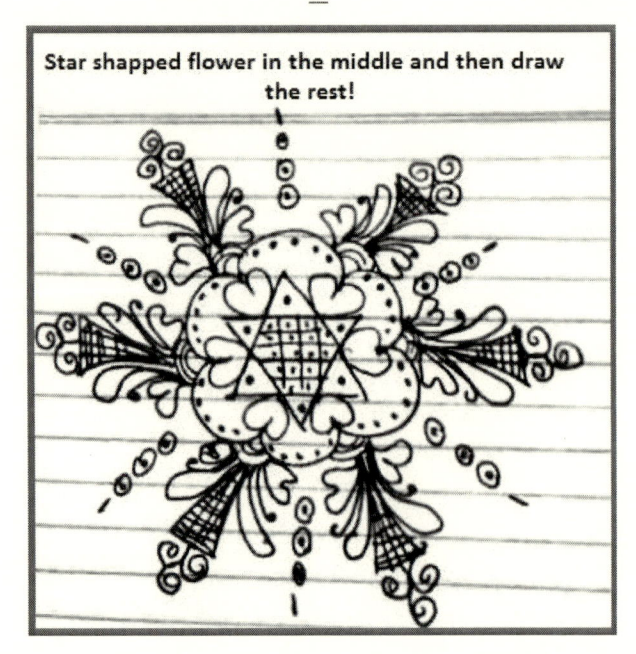

> Star shapped flower in the middle and then draw the rest!

- Star shaped flower in the middle with hearts. Then extended to other flowers in all the sides. No dots required and completely free hand kolam.
- Design can be changed to form any other pattern too!
- Center dots are just for decoration.

**Search "Ganapathy Upasana" & "Lord Hanuman Upasana" / "Varahi Upasana" in Kindle or Amazon to download for auspicious poojas!
Author: "G R Narasimhan"**

3

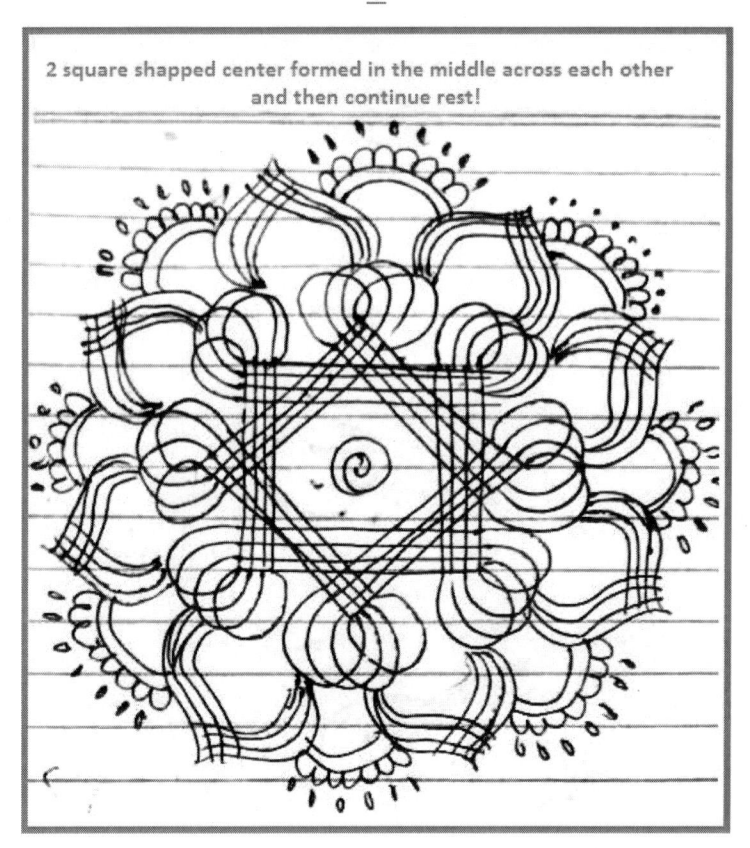

> 2 square shapped center formed in the middle across each other and then continue rest!

- Two square shapes in the center formed across each other. Then flower, petals and other patterns are formed around. Totally freehand rangoli with no dots.

4

- Complex type/ Advanced type rangoli where a small pattern like square shaped in the center and then further extended to form individual flower like shapes. Then the outer finishing shapes are drawn to give the perfect /completed kolam.

5

17 x 1 straight dots!

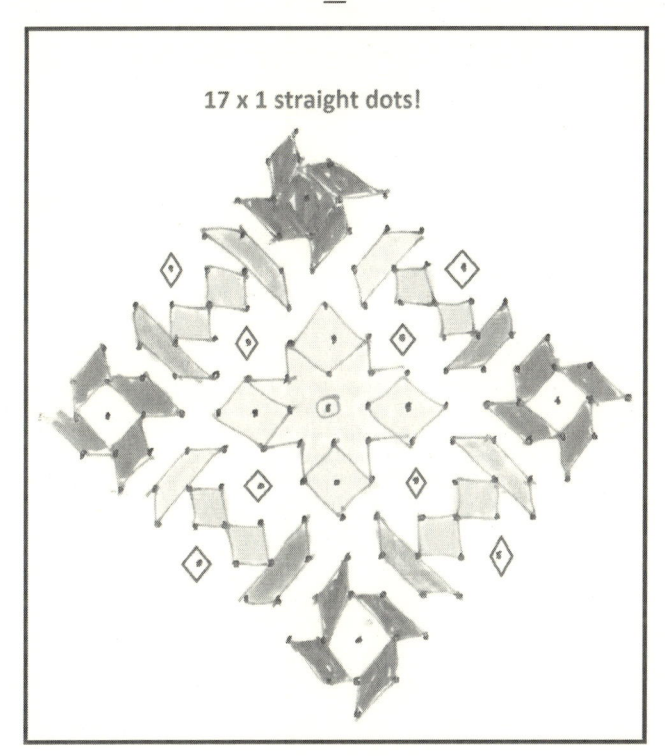

- 17 x 1 straight dots from the middle to top/bottom. Simply extended star in the middle and then followed by outer shapes.
- Free dots are covered with diamond shapes.

6

16 x 4 straight dots! middle to top/bottom/sides.

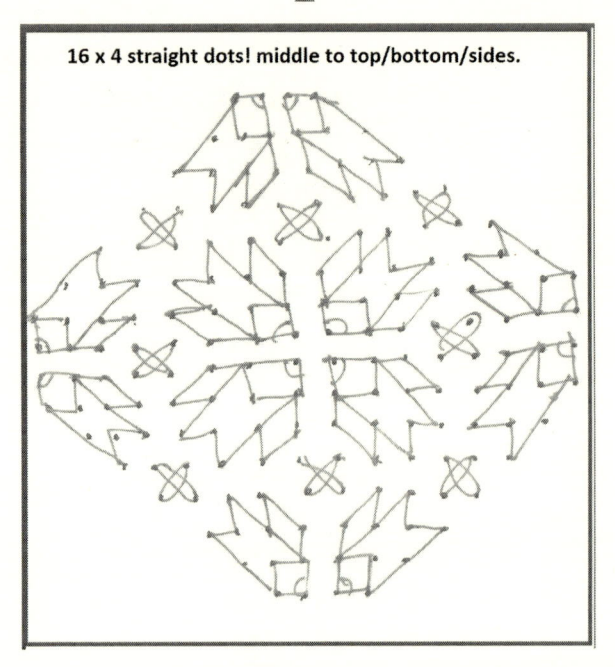

- Above rangoli with 16 x 4 straight dots from the middle to sides. Then fish shapes are formed from the middle to all the sides.

7

11 x 11 straight dots!

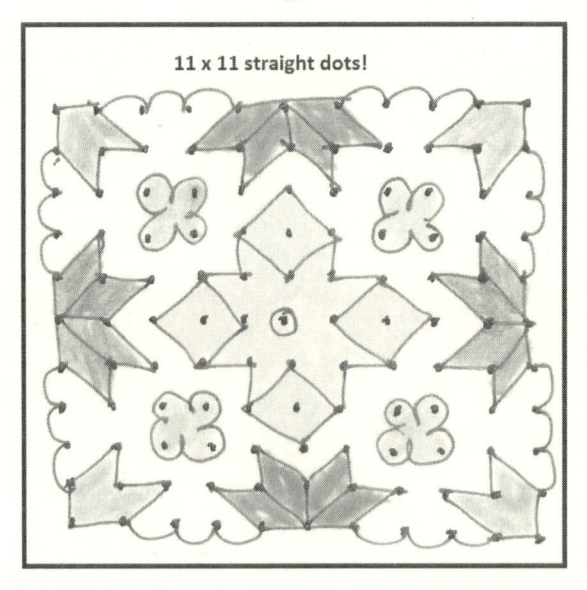

- 11 x 11 straight dots forms a star in the middle and extended to other shapes.

8

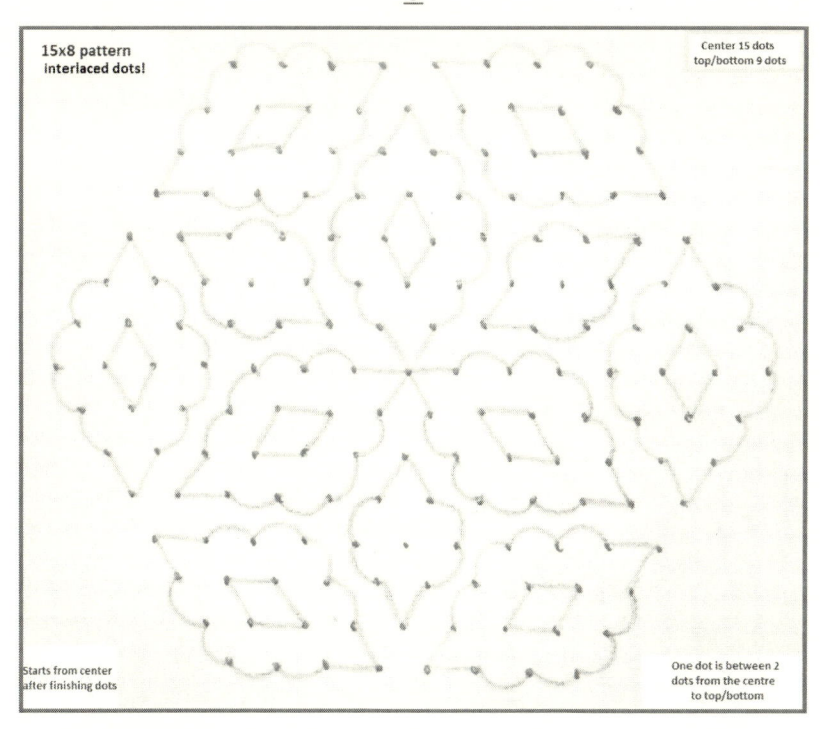

15x8 pattern interlaced dots!

Center 15 dots top/bottom 9 dots

Starts from center after finishing dots

One dot is between 2 dots from the centre to top/bottom

- 15 x 8 interlaced dots pattern.
- Center is having 15 dots and 8 dots top/bottom from the center.
- One dot is between two dots just forms interlaced pattern.
- Stars from the center and then flower based patterns all sides.

**Search "Ganapathy Upasana" & "Lord Hanuman Upasana" / "Varahi Upasana" in Kindle or Amazon to download for auspicious poojas!
Author: "G R Narasimhan"**

9

9 x 9 straight dots!

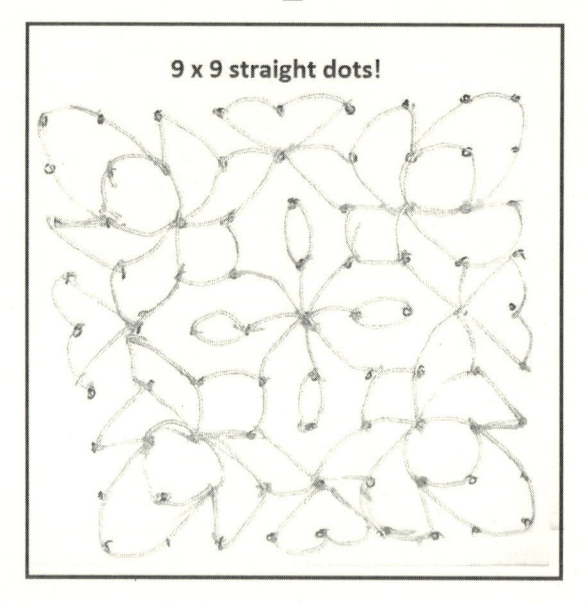

- 9 x 9 straight dots; initially from the center, a flower like design drawn.
- Then bunch of flowers are drawn in all corners and connected.

10

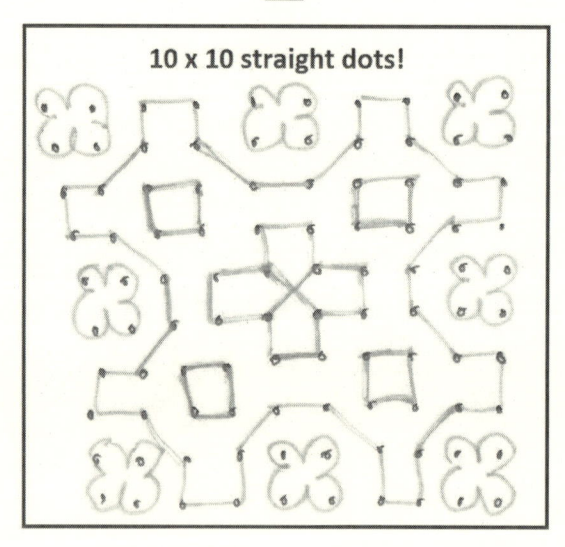

10 x 10 straight dots!

- 10 x 10 dots are in straight lines. A cross shape if drawn in the middle and then followed by four squares.
- Then the other shapes like flowers are made in all sides.

11

15 x 8 interlaced dots!

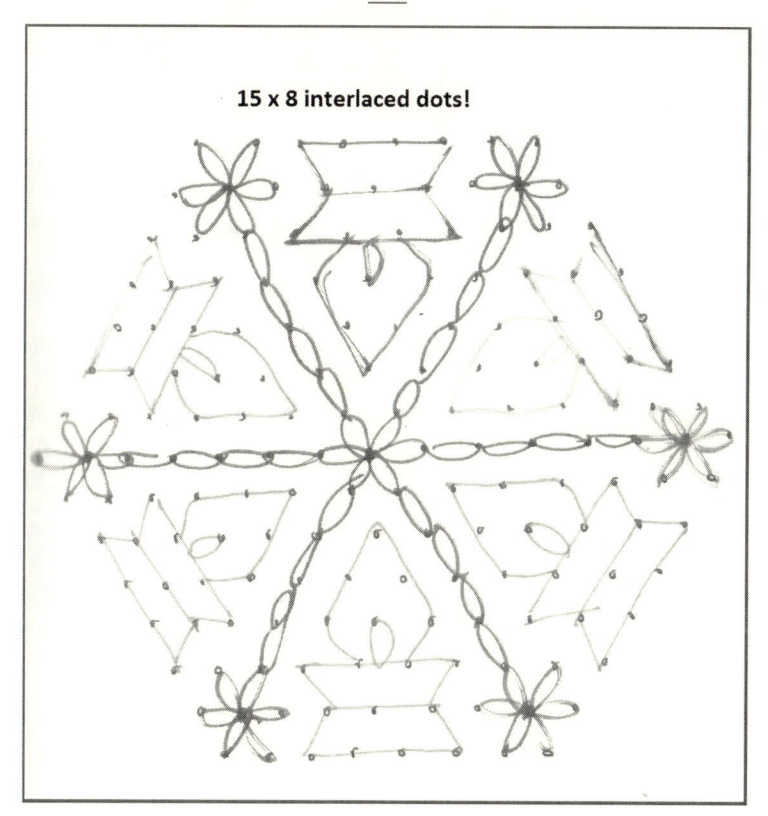

- 15 x 8 interlaced dots are arranged from middle to bottom/top.
- Chain like shape is drawn from the center to corners.
- Then lamps are drawn on sides.

12

15 x 3 straight dots! Middle to all sides.

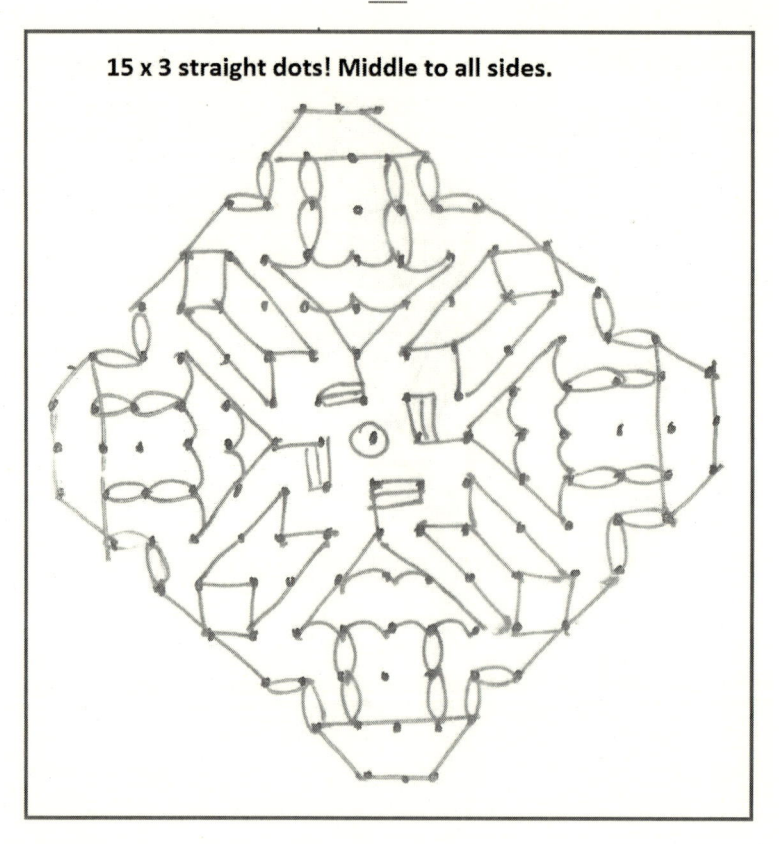

- 15 x 3 dots in straight line from the center.
- Then boat/ Chariot with flag like design/ pattern are drawn in all sides.
- In-between fish symbol is given.

13

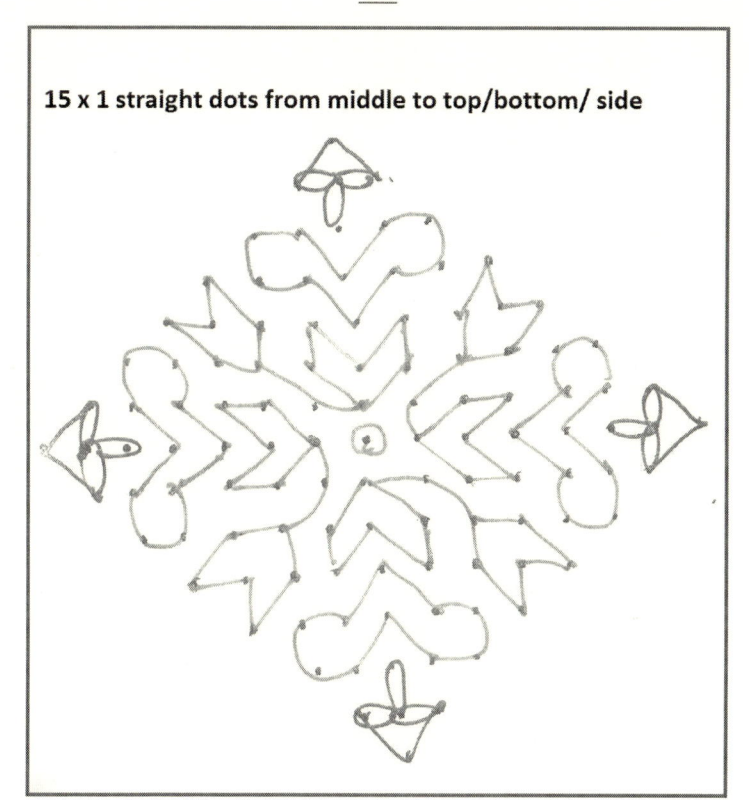

15 x 1 straight dots from middle to top/bottom/ side

- The above kolam has 15 x 1 straight dots from the middle to all sides.
- Lamp shapes with different pattern is given.
- Center dot is covered with a small circle.

Search "Ganapathy Upasana" & "Lord Hanuman Upasana" / "Varahi Upasana" in Kindle or Amazon to download for auspicious poojas!
Author: "G R Narasimhan"

14

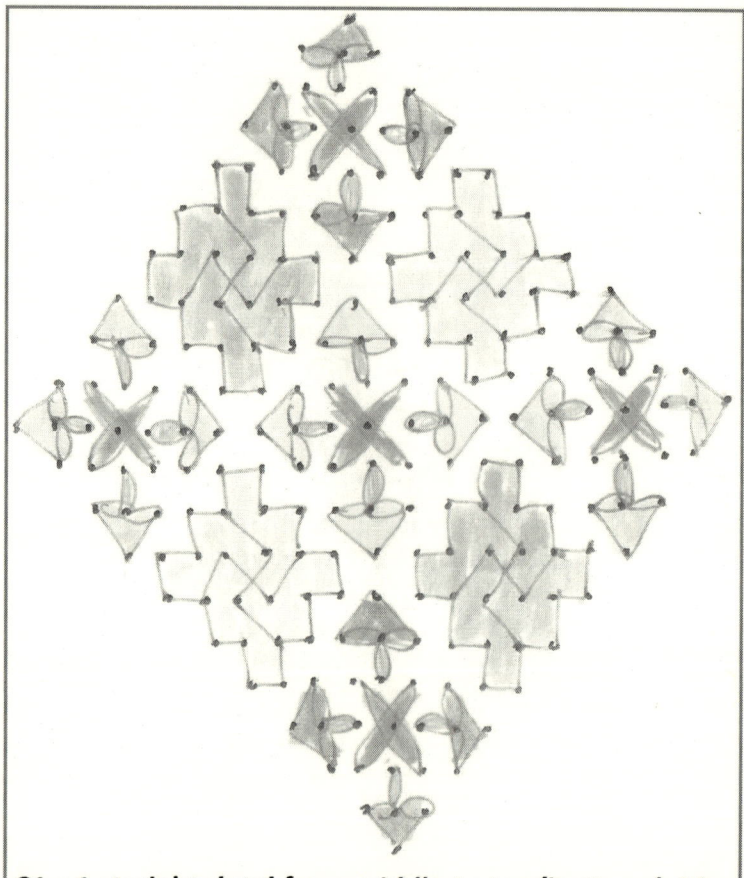

21 x 1 straight dots! from middle to top/bottom/ sides.

- 21 x 1 straight dots are from the middle to sides.
- Center portion with a cross curved shape with four lamps.
- Similar pattern are to 4 sides as well.
- Also four cross shaped pattern given in the middle of four sides.

15

15 x 1 straight dots!

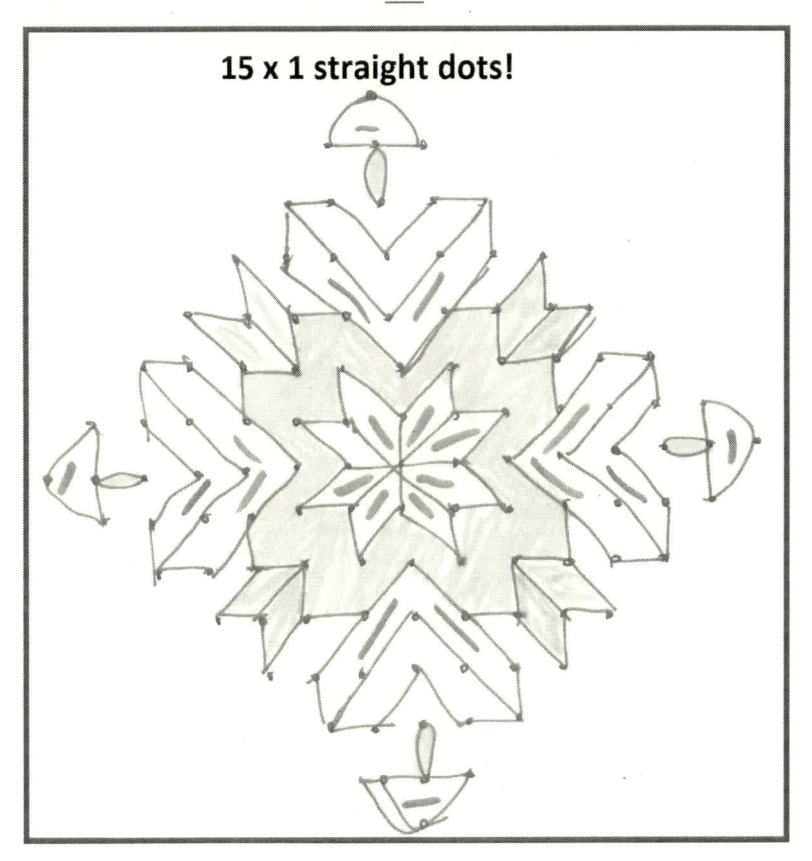

- Here 15 x 1 straight dots are given from middle to all sides.
- Then star pattern in the middle and then V pattern above one level.
- Finally finished with 4 lamps in 4 sides.

16

15 x 3 Straight dots! from middle to bottom/top

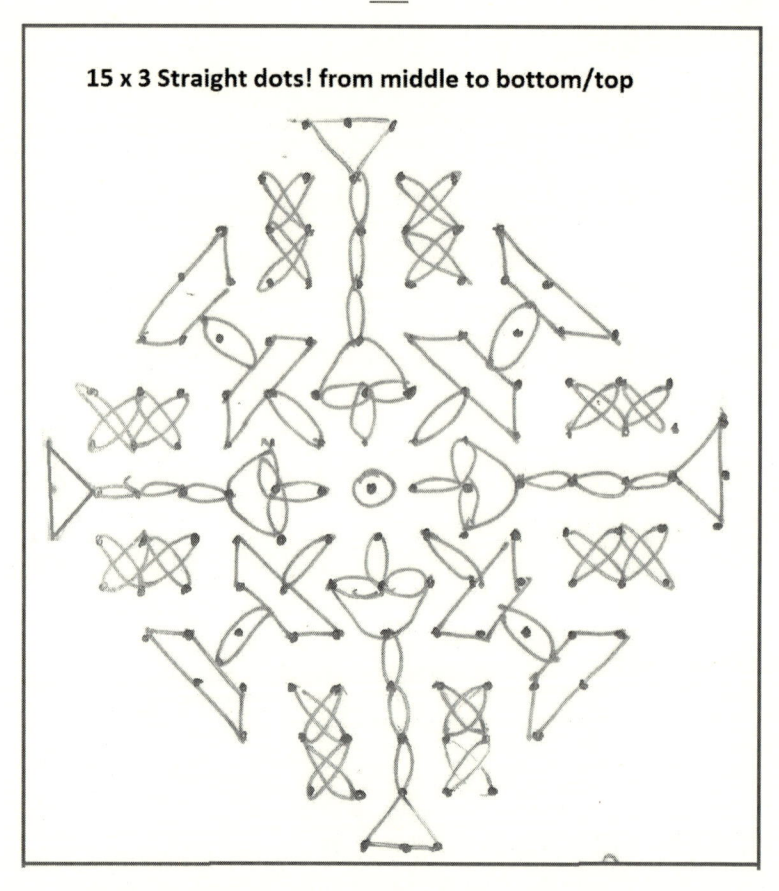

- 15 x 3 straight dots drawn from middle to top/ bottom.
- Then starting from the center the different shapes of auspicious lamps are drawn.
- Double cross covers the lamp sides.

17

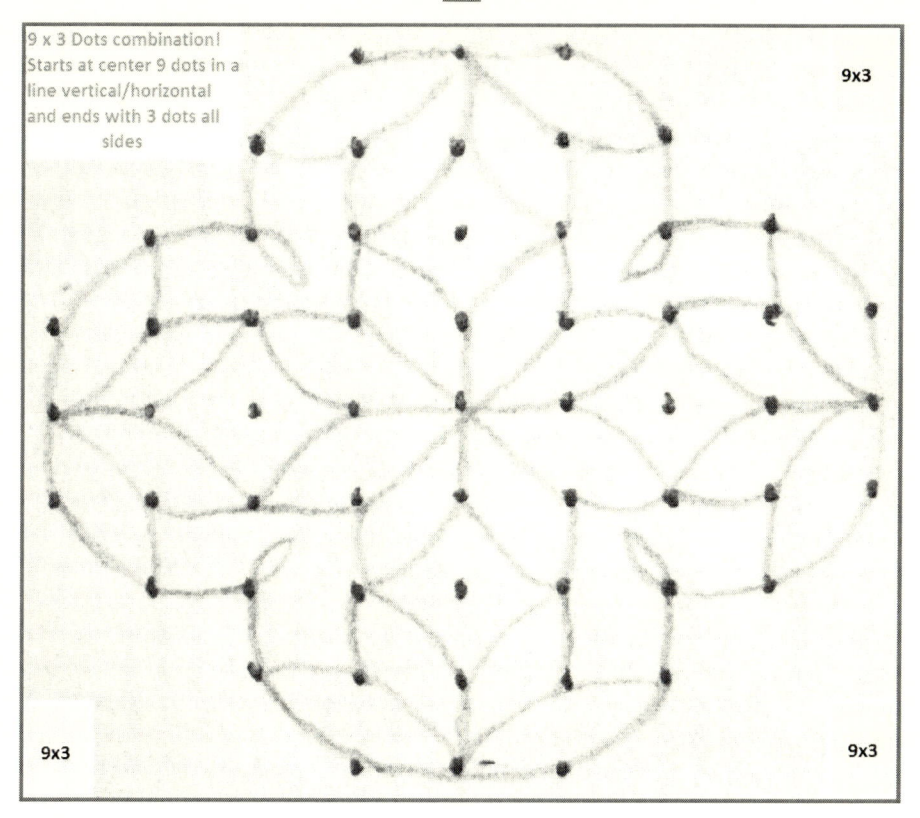

9 x 3 Dots combination! Starts at center 9 dots in a line vertical/horizontal and ends with 3 dots all sides

9x3

9x3

9x3

- 9 x 3 dots in straight line from the middle.
- Star or flower shaped design in the middle area and then extended to shape up the other patterns like bowl.

18

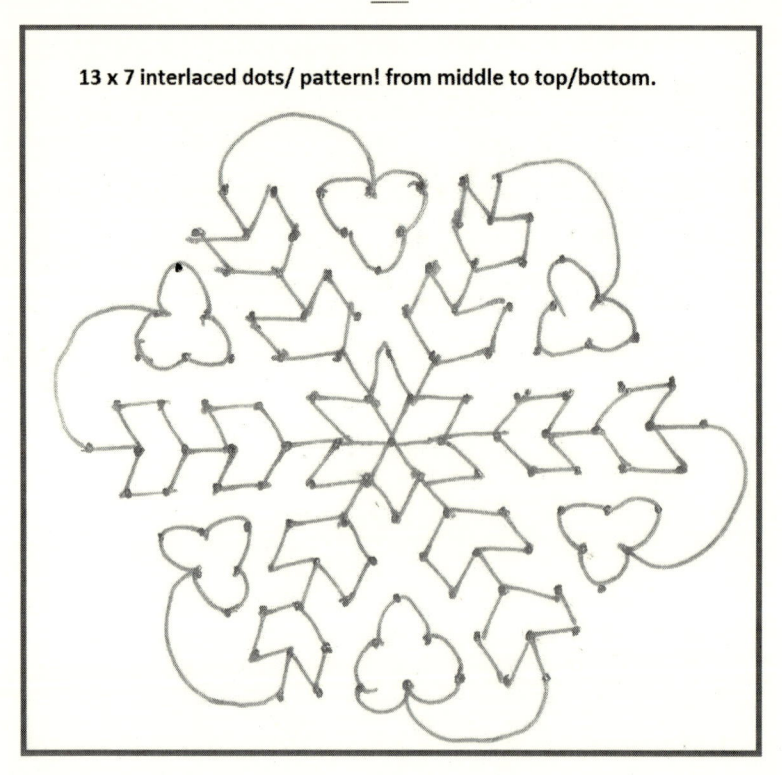

13 x 7 interlaced dots/ pattern! from middle to top/bottom.

- This advanced pattern has 13 x 7 interlaced dots from the middle to top and bottom.

- Triangle shaped pattern in the middle and then extended to flower patterns.

19

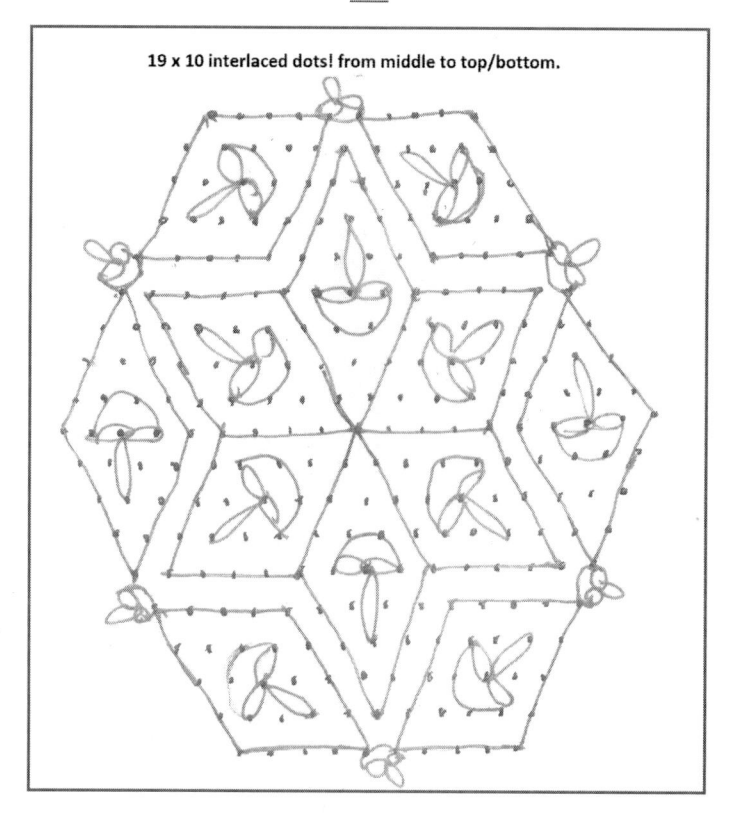

19 x 10 interlaced dots! from middle to top/bottom.

- Above one is 19 x 10 interlaced pattern of dots.
- Draw a star shaped lines from the middle to finish primary part.
- Then diamond shapes with lamps as shown.

20

13 x 7 interlaced dots! from middle to top/bottom!

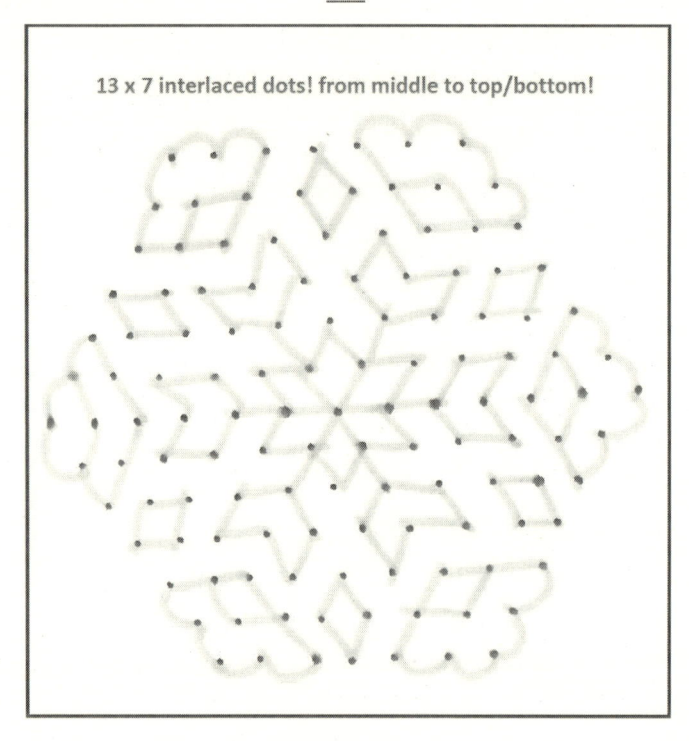

- 13 x 7 interlaced dots from middle to top/bottom.

- Then from the center; the star shape is drawn and extended to have cloud/flower pattern.

Search "Ganapathy Upasana" & "Lord Hanuman Upasana" / "Varahi Upasana" in Kindle or Amazon to download for auspicious poojas!
Author: "G R Narasimhan"

21

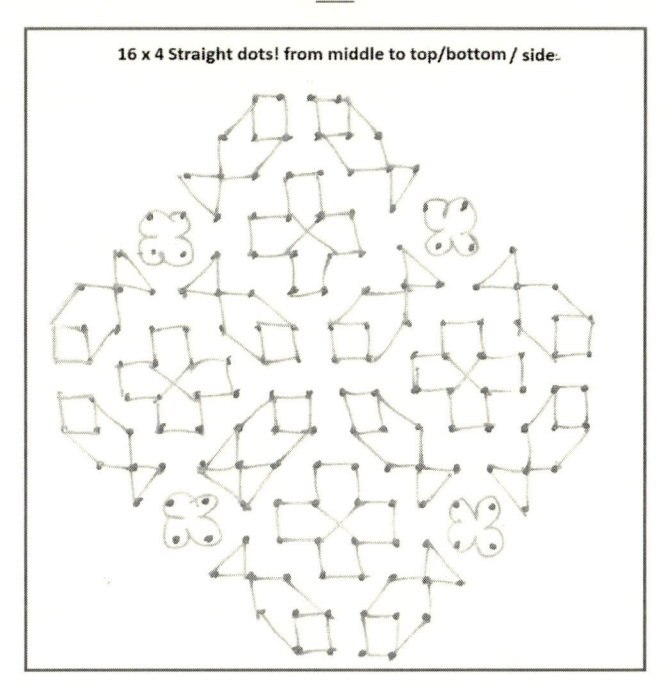

16 x 4 Straight dots! from middle to top/bottom / side

- 16 x 4 straight dots fro center 4 lines to sides. Then cross and fish shaped patterns completed.

22

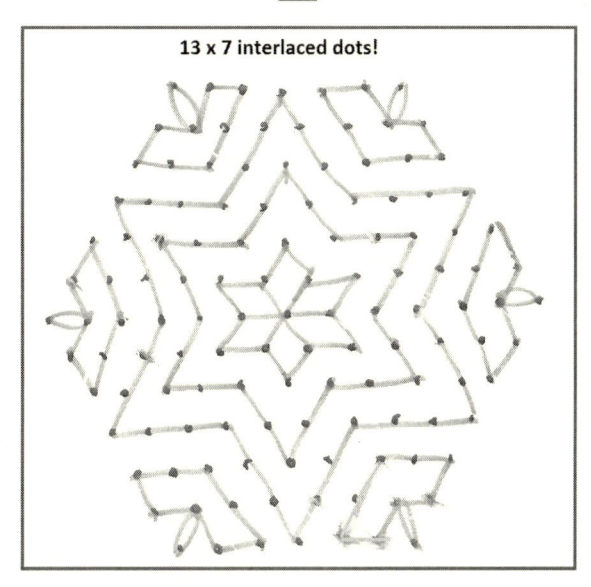

13 x 7 interlaced dots!

- 13 x 7 interlaced dots forming a star shape in the middle to top and followed by lamp finishing in the sides.

23

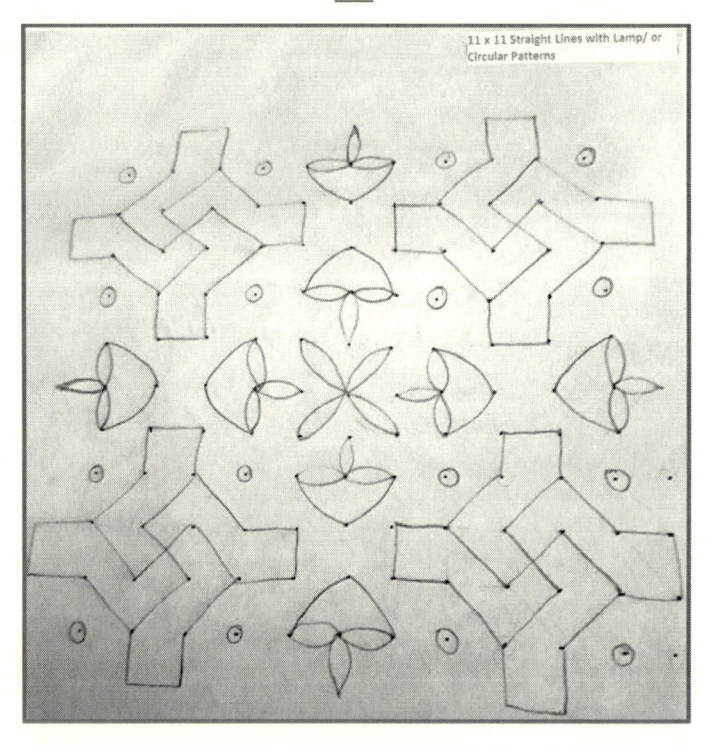

- 11 x 11 straight lines to form cross, circular and lamp shapes along with.

24

- 17 x 9 interlaced points to form a star in the middle and other covered stars. Sides are with lamp shaped design.

25

13 x 7 interlaced dots! from middle to top/bottom.

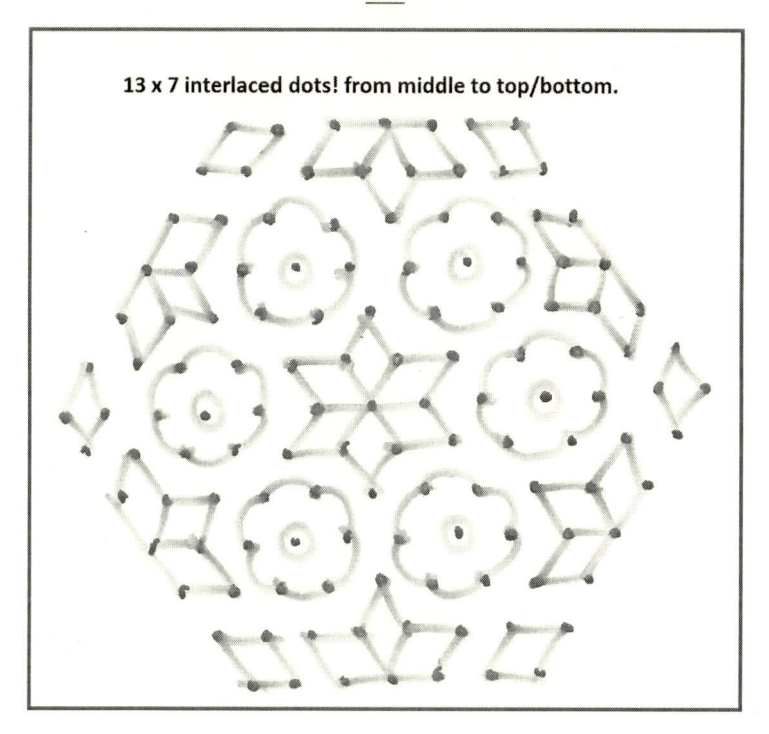

- 13 x 7 interlaced dots from center to top/ bottom.
- Then middle star pattern with flowers around.
- Boat and diamond shapes; finally finishing the kolam.

26

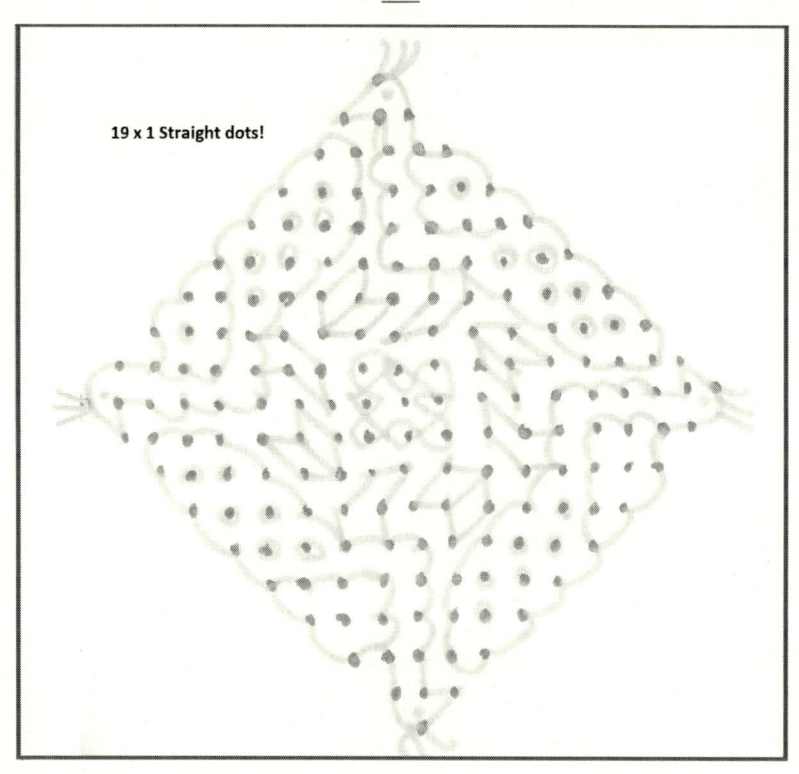

- 19 x 1 straight dots from the middle to sides.
- Small curved design in the middle and then small flags around.
- Outer is completely with peacock 4 sides.

27

13 x 7 interlaced dots!

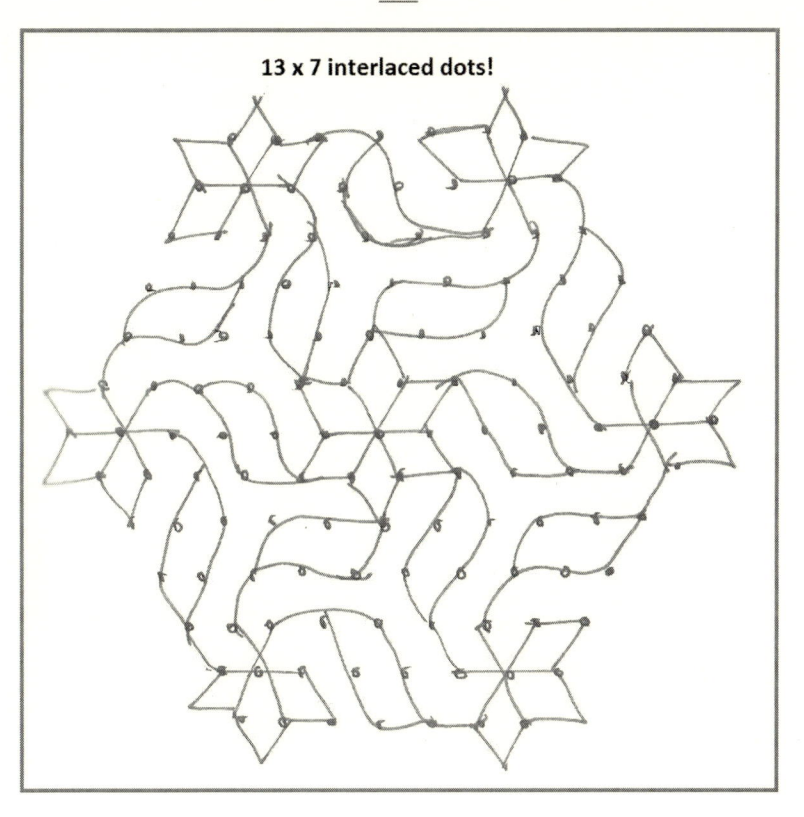

- 13 x 7 interlaced dots from the middle to top/bottom.
- Then a star shaped pattern in the middle is extended to form other stars in and around.

28

13 x 7 interlaced dots!

- 13 x 7 interlaced dots from the middle to top/bottom.
- Then a star shaped pattern in the middle is extended to form other heart and diamonds with flowers in and around.

29

13 x 7 interlaced dots!

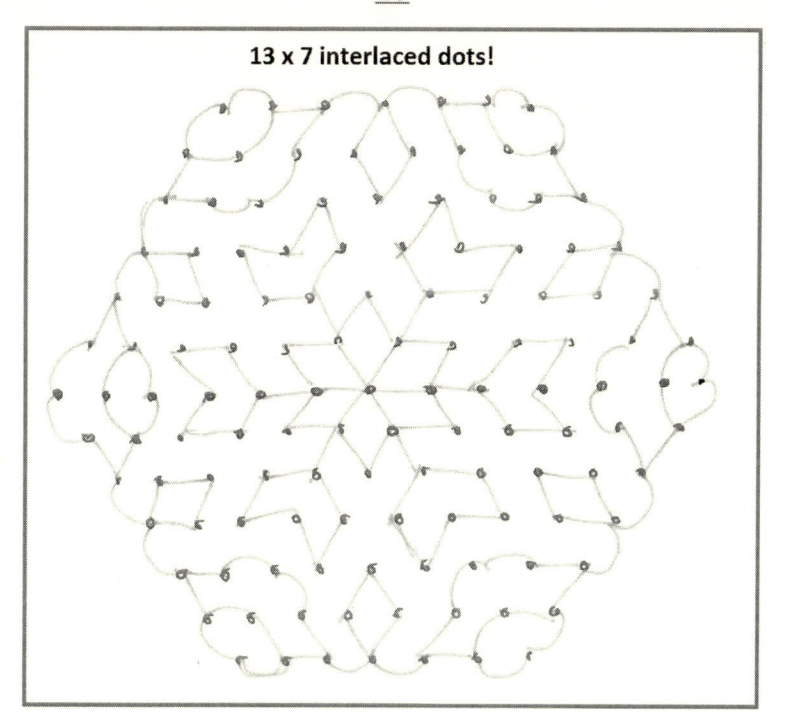

- 13 x 7 interlaced dots from the middle to top/bottom.
- Then a star shaped pattern in the middle is extended to form other diamonds and bowls in and around.

30

19 x 3 straight dots from middle to top/ bottom/ sides!

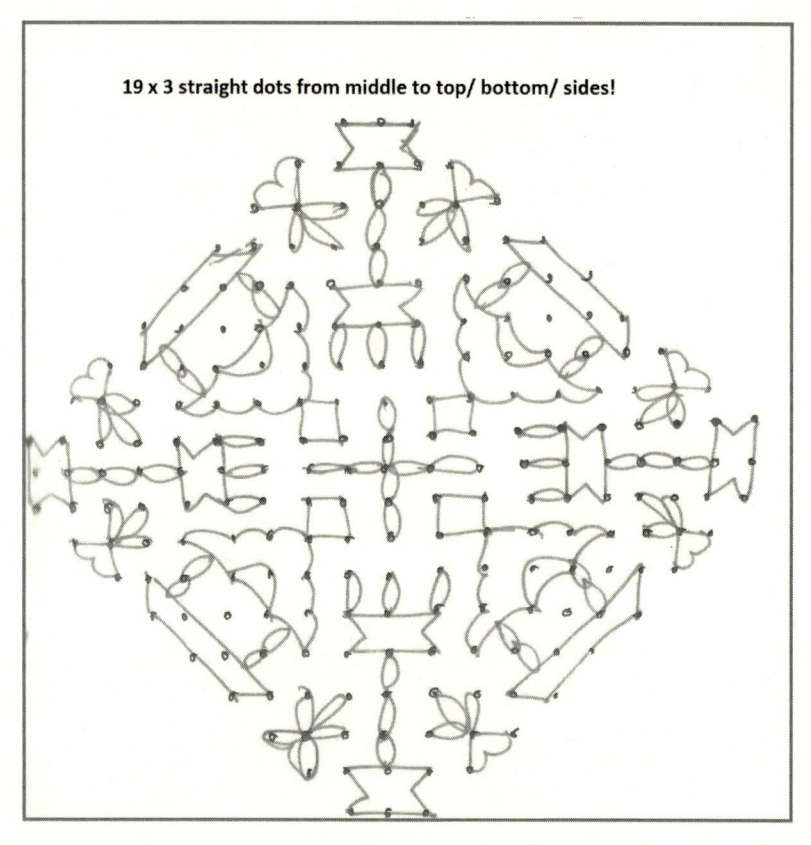

- 19 x 3 straight dots from the middle to top/bottom.
- Then a star shaped pattern in the middle is extended to form other patterns.
- Then chariot and lamps are drawn in outer sides.

31

15 x 8 interlaced points! from middle to top/bottom.

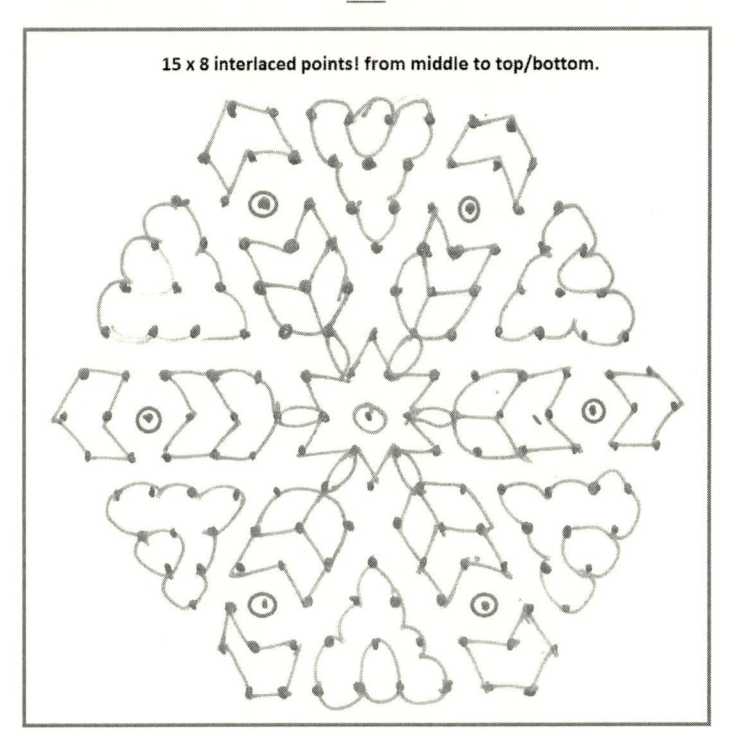

- 15 x 8 interlaced dots from the middle to top/bottom.
- Then a star shaped pattern in the middle is extended to form other flowers and conical shapes in and around.

32

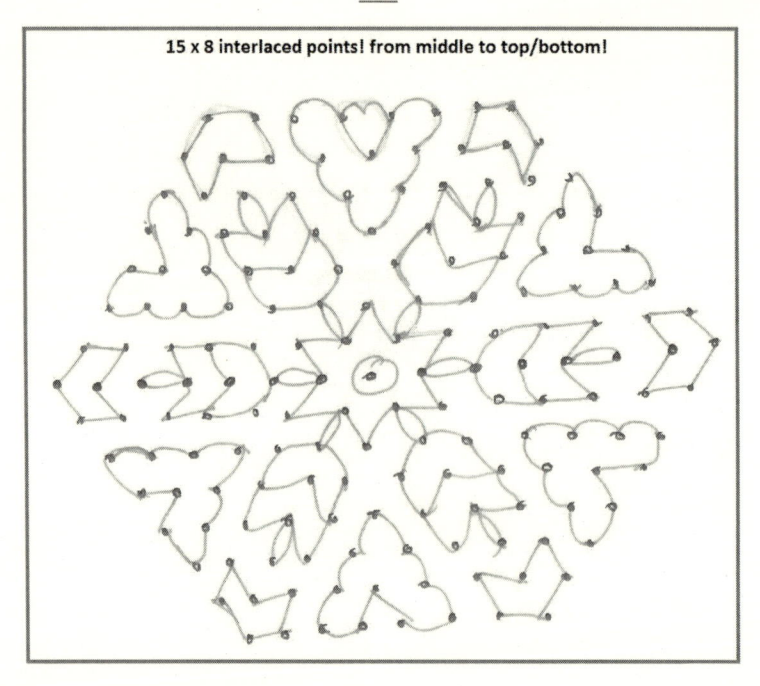

15 x 8 interlaced points! from middle to top/bottom!

- Similar to the previous one.
- 15 x 8 interlaced dots from the middle to top/bottom.
- Then a star shaped pattern in the middle is extended to form other flowers and conical shapes in and around.

Search "Ganapathy Upasana" & "Lord Hanuman Upasana" / "Varahi Upasana" in Kindle or Amazon to download for auspicious poojas!
Author: "G R Narasimhan"

33

caption in image: 13 x 7 interlaced points! from middle to top & bottom!

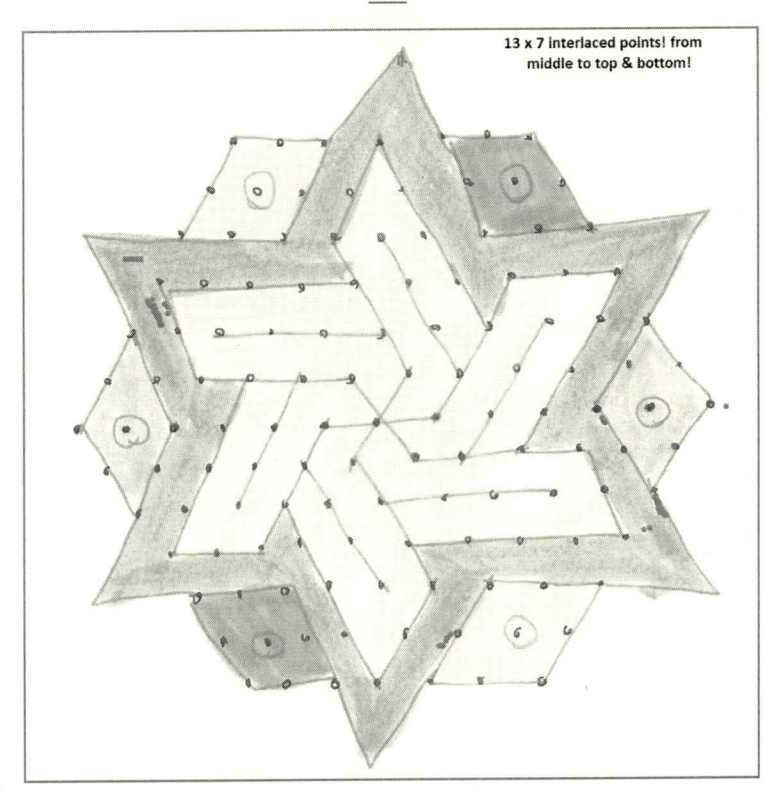

- 13 x 7 interlaced dots from the middle to top/bottom.
- Then a star shaped pattern in the middle is extended to form other stars and diamond in and around.

34

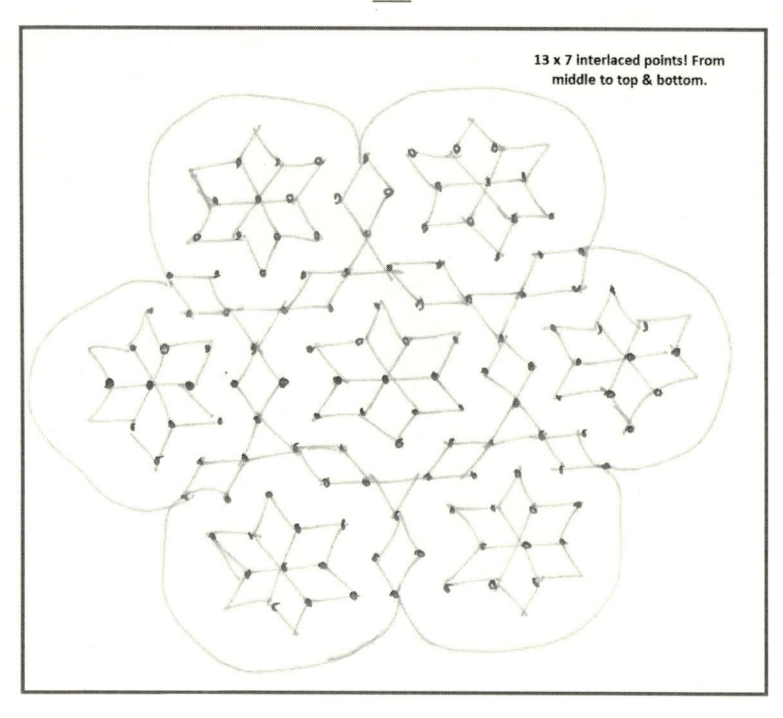

13 x 7 interlaced points! From middle to top & bottom.

- 13 x 7 interlaced dots from the middle to top/bottom.
- Then a star shaped pattern in the middle is extended to form other stars and circular outer shapes.

Search "Ganapathy Upasana" & "Lord Hanuman Upasana" / "Varahi Upasana" in Kindle or Amazon to download for auspicious poojas!
Author: "G R Narasimhan"

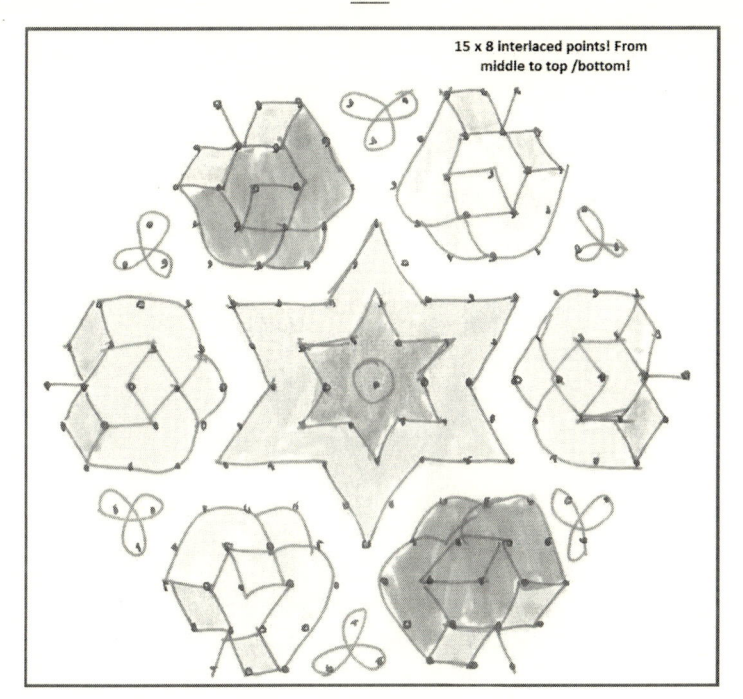

35

- 15 x 8 interlaced dots from the middle to top/bottom.
- Then a star shaped pattern in the middle is extended to form other stars and flowers with bees' shapes in and around.

36

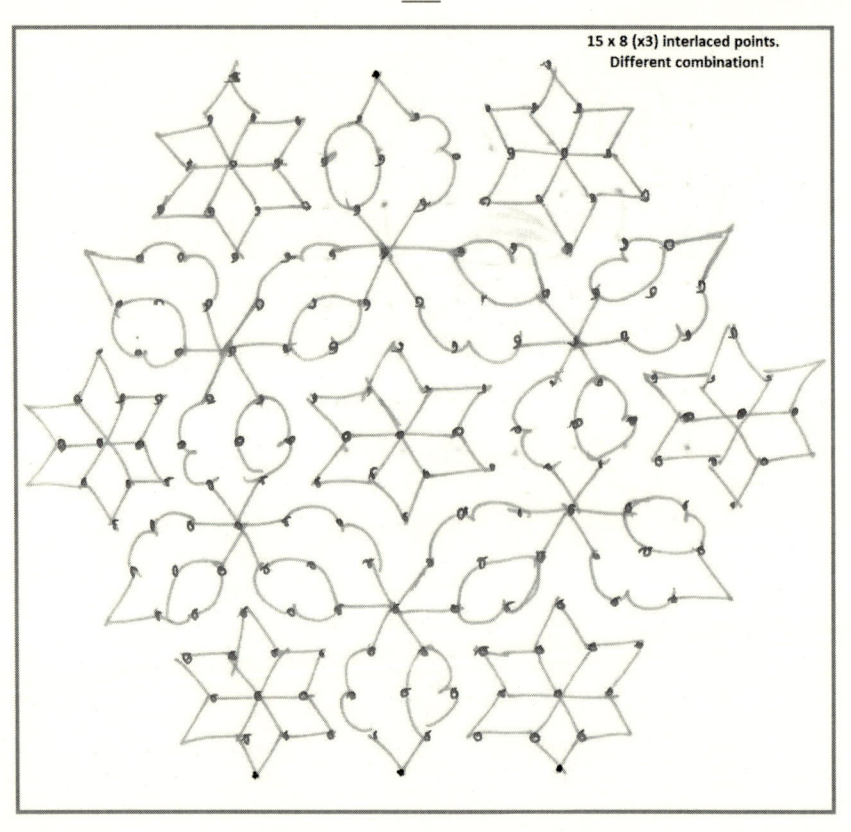

15 x 8 (x3) interlaced points.
Different combination!

- 15 x 8 (x3) interlaced dots from the middle to top/bottom.
- Then a star shaped pattern in the middle is extended to form other flowers and stars in and around.
- Also sangu shapes around the star.

37

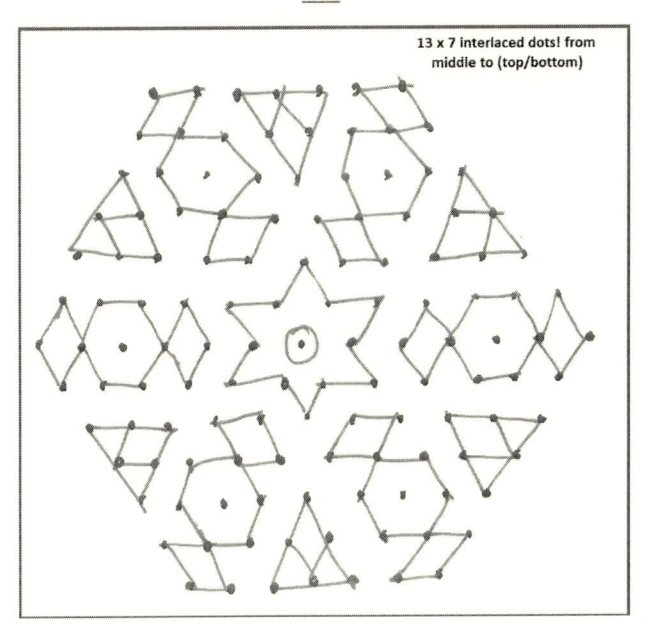

- 13 x 7 interlaced dots from the middle to top/bottom.
- Then a star shaped pattern in the middle is extended to form other triangles and hexogens.

38

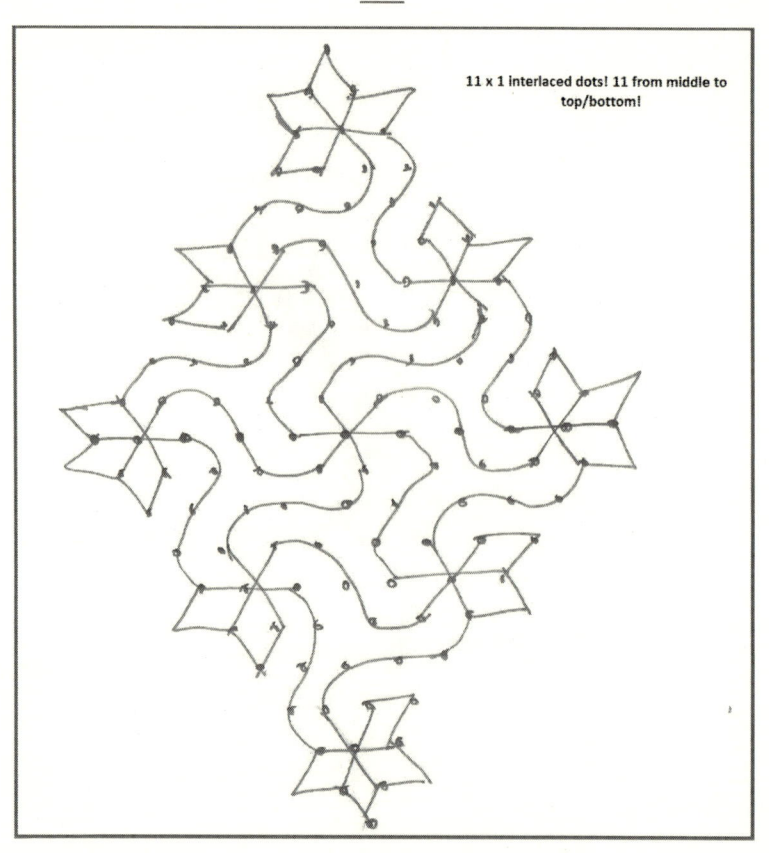

11 x 1 interlaced dots! 11 from middle to top/bottom!

- 11 x 1 interlaced dots from the middle to top/bottom.
- Then a galaxy shaped pattern in the middle is extended to form other stars in and around.

**Search "Ganapathy Upasana" & "Lord Hanuman Upasana" / "Varahi Upasana" in Kindle or Amazon to download for auspicious poojas!
Author: "G R Narasimhan"**

39

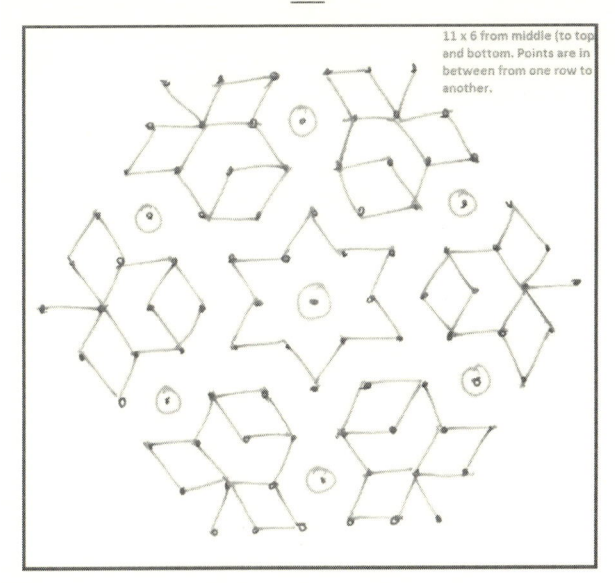

11 x 6 from middle (to top and bottom. Points are in between from one row to another.

- 11 x 6 interlaced dots from the middle to top/bottom.
- Then a star shaped pattern in the middle is extended to form other satellite shapes in and around. Free dots are covered with small circles.

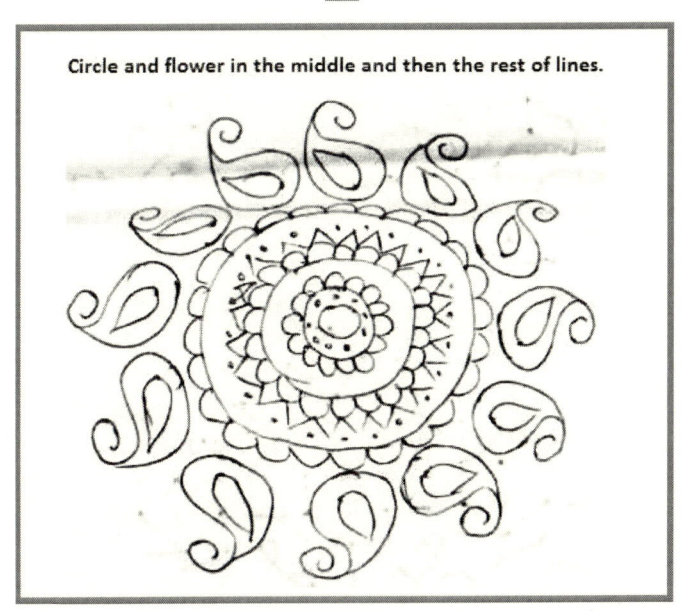

40

Circle and flower in the middle and then the rest of lines.

- Freehand advanced type rangoli is shown above. Similar one in medium category also. First 2 circles in the center and then flower shape is drawn. Then other designs were completed. Can be extended to any other patterns.

Chapter Four – Extra Patterns

This extras rangoli section covers many patterns with or without dots for your reference. All are hand drawn rangolis/kolams only. Based on the given designs, you can form or draw your own style rangoli by yourself. No description is given in this section. Please go ahead with your observation.

<u>1</u>

<u>2</u>

3

4

5

6

7

8

9

10

11

12

13

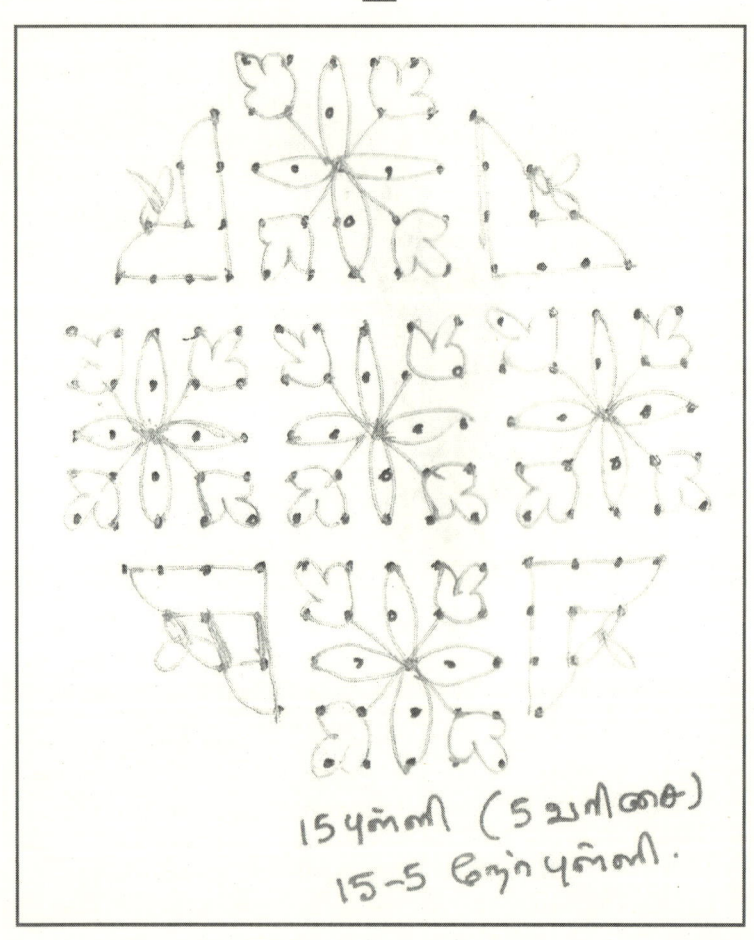

15 புள்ளி (5 வரிசை)
15-5 நேர் புள்ளி.

14

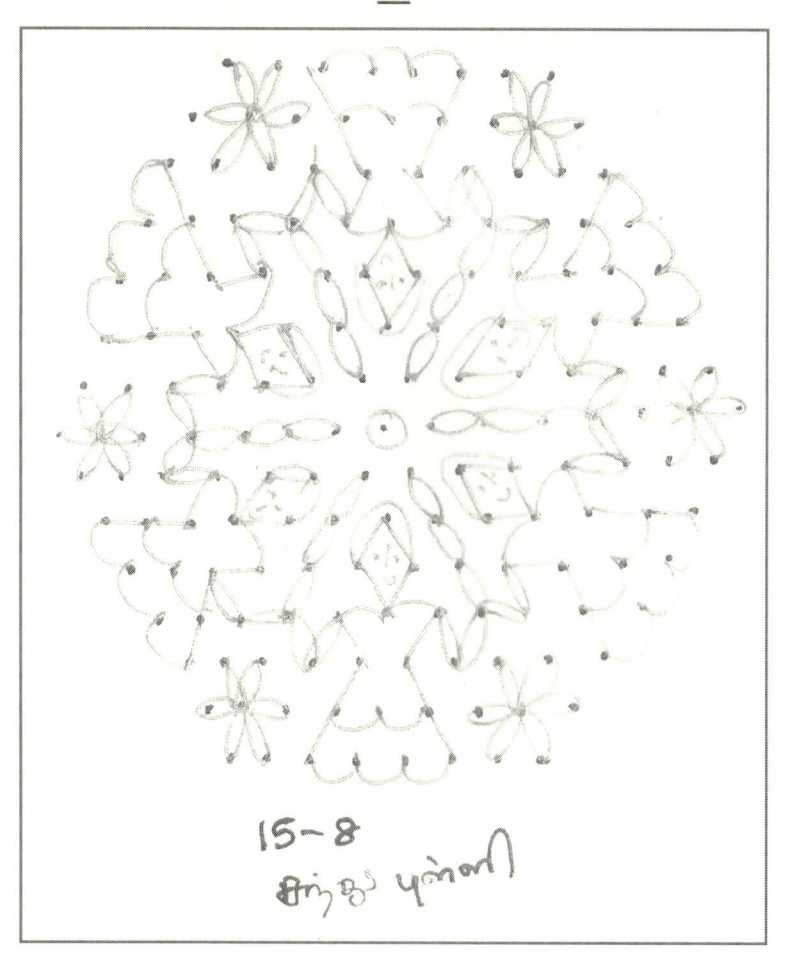

15-8
சிந்து புள்ளி

Search "Ganapathy Upasana" & "Lord Hanuman Upasana" / "Varahi Upasana" in Kindle or Amazon to download for auspicious poojas!
Author: "G R Narasimhan"

15

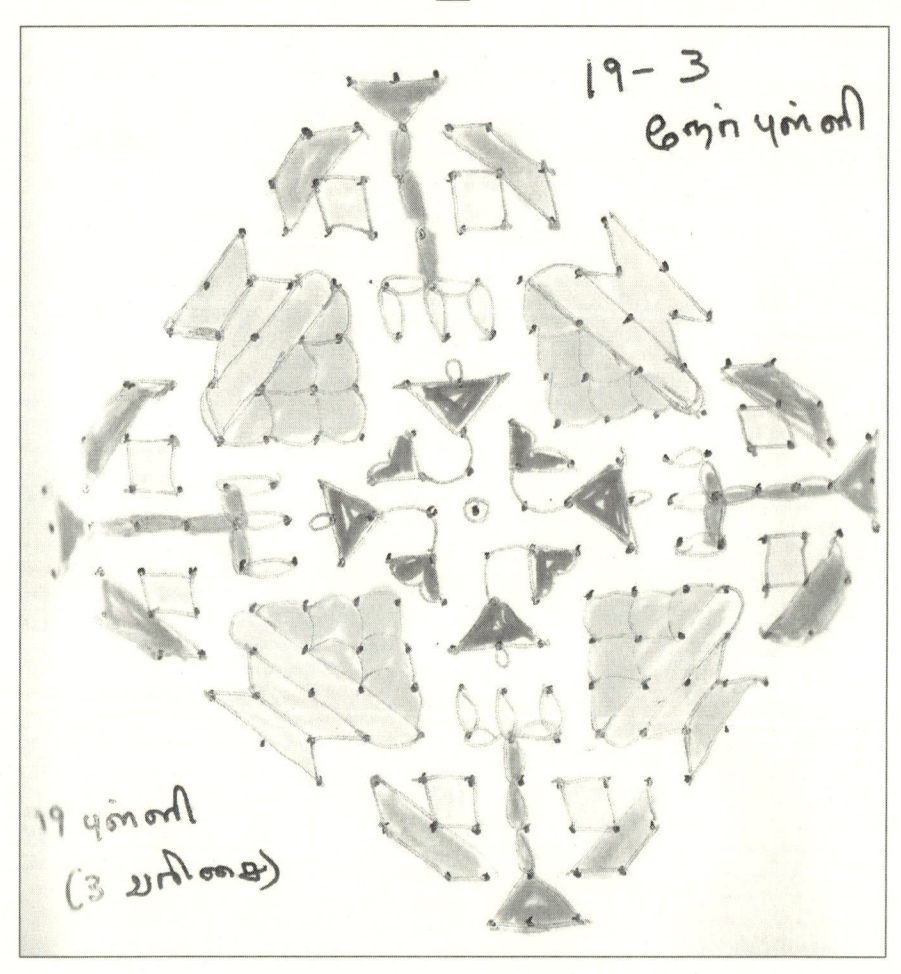

19-3
நேர் புள்ளி

19 புள்ளி
(3 பரிசை)

16

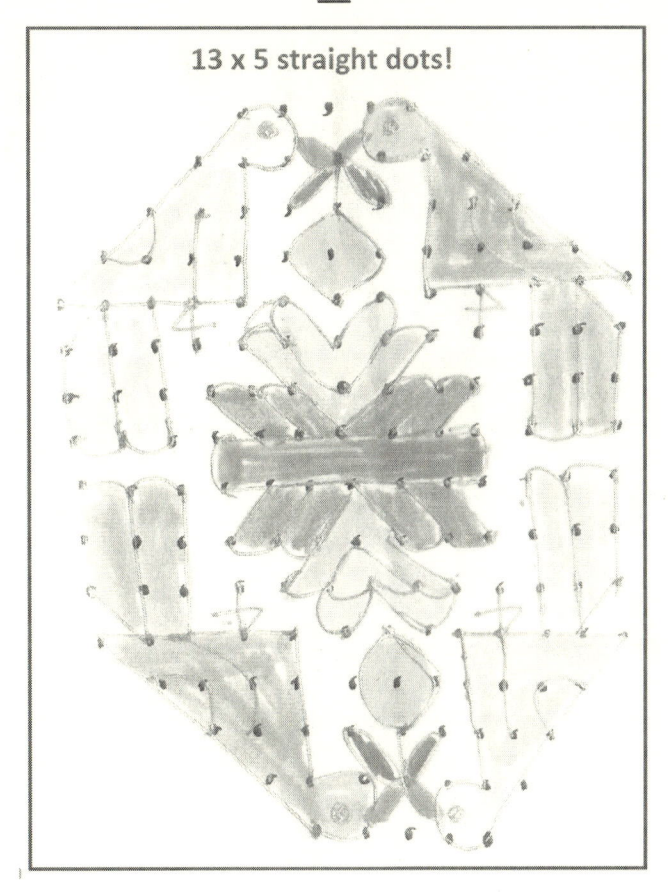

13 x 5 straight dots!

17

17 x 1 straight dots!

18

94

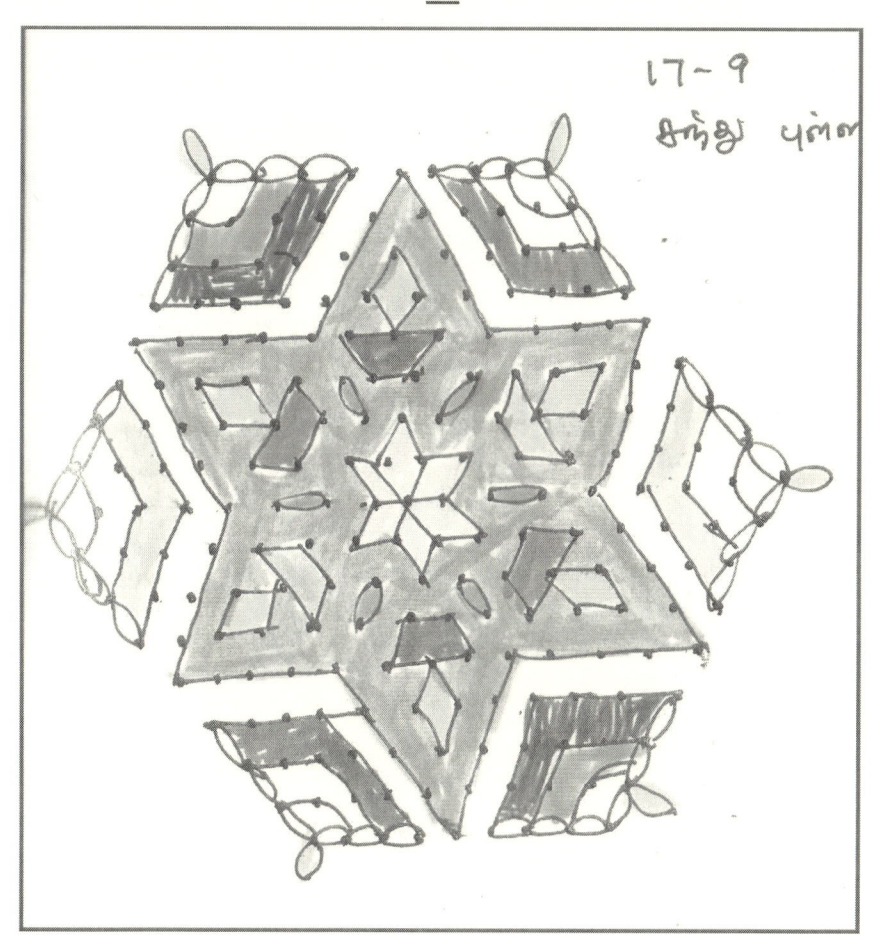

Search "Ganapathy Upasana" & "Lord Hanuman Upasana" / "Varahi Upasana" in Kindle or Amazon to download for auspicious poojas!
Author: "G R Narasimhan"

20

21

22

23

24

25

My pen Rangoli

26

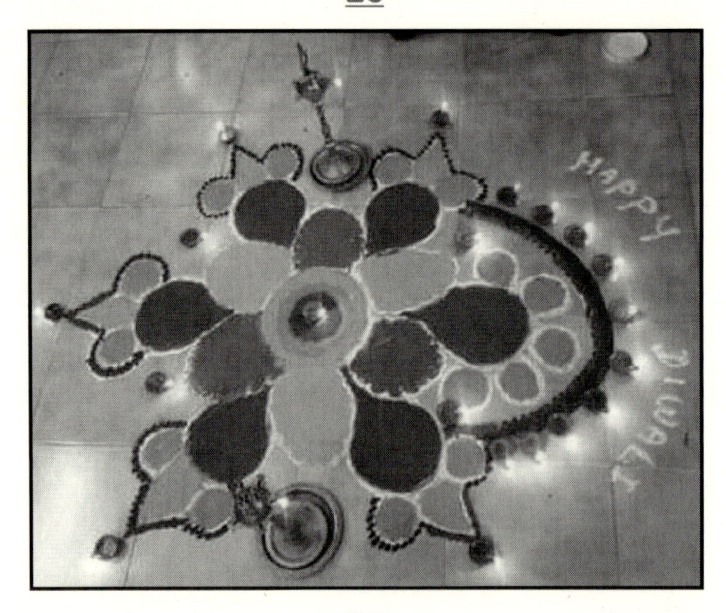

27

100

28

Search "MBA Basics in 24 Hours" in Kindle or Amazon to download all the 8 + 2 Basic MBA chapters & Additional Books!

Author: "G R Narasimhan"

29

15 x 9 interlaced dots!

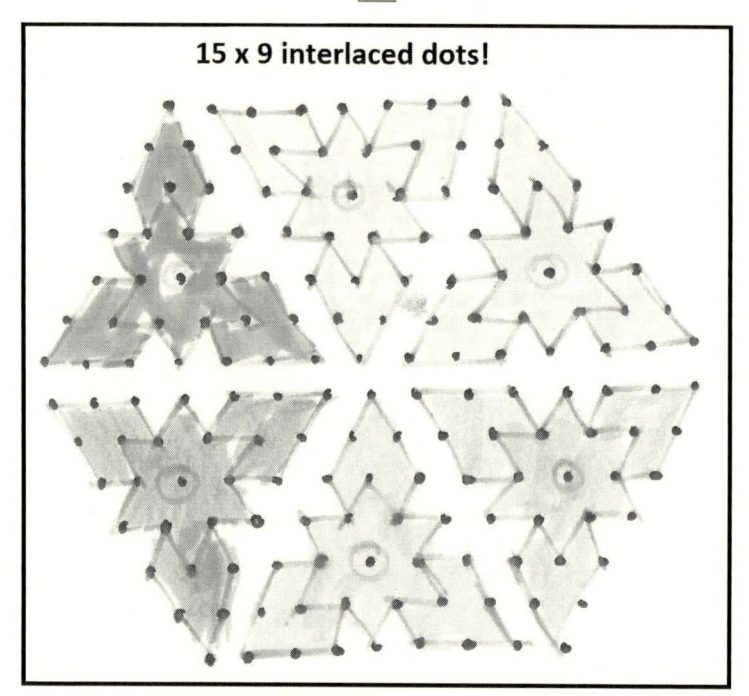

30

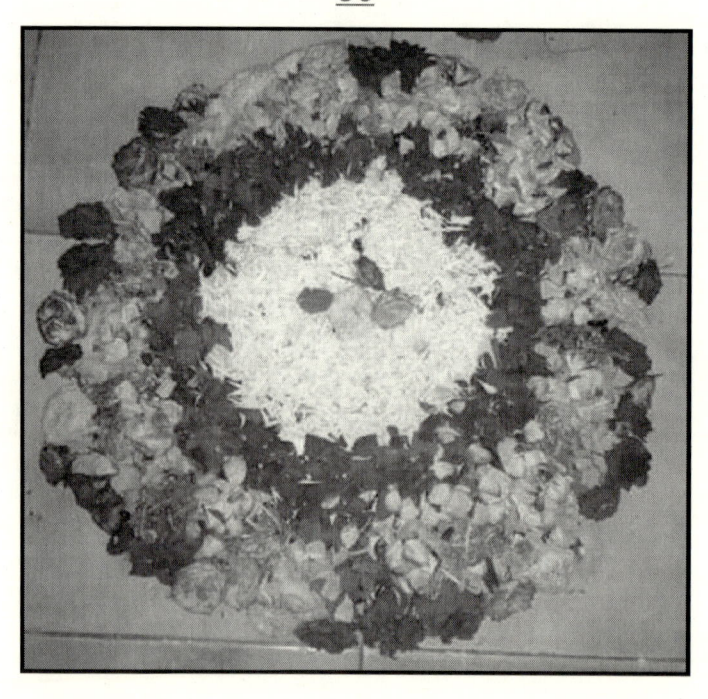

31

Search "MBA Basics in 24 Hours" in Kindle or Amazon to download all the 8 + 2 Basic MBA chapters & Additional Books!

Author: "G R Narasimhan"

32

33

CONCLUSION & THANKS NOTE!

- This rangoli book covers more than hundred patterns which was in to three major categories like basic, medium (intermediate) and advanced for anyone to start with simple to complex levels.
- Nowadays as people are living in small flats or shared accommodation due to the family split and poverty in India; people are not having enough space to draw rangoli/ kolams. Another reason is busy schedule!
- Some homemakers are still practicing this in the pooja room or prayer/ meditation rools or in the small doorsteps. Really good.
- Temples and other holy places are still decorated with simple to complex types of kolams/ muggulu.
- From normal rice flour to colour powders are used to showcase colourful patterns and designs.
- Sometimes to keep these kolam patterns permanently; paints are used.
- Home interiors and curtains, windows etc are still using these designs to attract wealth and prosperity.
- During any pooja or festival time as described in the introduction section; rangoli patterns used.
- We tried very much to give natural hand drawn patterns in this book without any computerized printing.
- From children to elders, male or female; anyone can practice rangoli to improve their art skills.
- I am very much thankful to my wife, cousins and friends who supported very well by sharing their kolams and helped me to finish this book with fully handmade type.

For any feedback, query or suggestions please mail to astronara@gmail.com or info@zodiacservices.net.

You can also contact via www.zodiacservices.net/contact.

THANK YOU!

Made in United States
North Haven, CT
22 January 2022